TRUTH, MORALITY, AND MEANING IN HISTORY

In this important new book, Paul T. Phillips argues that most professional historians – aside from a relatively small number devoted to theory and methodology – have concerned themselves with particular, specialized areas of research, thereby ignoring the fundamental questions of truth, morality, and meaning. This is less so in the thriving general community of history enthusiasts beyond academia, and may explain, in part at least, history's sharp decline as a subject of choice by students in recent years.

Phillips sees great dangers resulting from the thinking of extreme relativists and postmodernists on the futility of attaining historical truth, especially in the age of "post-truth." He also believes that moral judgment and the search for meaning in history should be considered part of the discipline's mandate. In each section of this study, Phillips outlines the nature of individual issues and past efforts to address them, including approaches derived from other disciplines. This book is a call to action for all those engaged in the study of history to direct more attention to the fundamental questions of truth, morality, and meaning.

(UTP Insights)

PAUL T. PHILLIPS is a senior research professor and professor emeritus in the Department of History at St Francis Xavier University.

UTP insights

UTP Insights is an innovative collection of brief books offering accessible introductions to the ideas that shape our world. Each volume in the series focuses on a contemporary issue, offering a fresh perspective anchored in scholarship. Spanning a broad range of disciplines in the social sciences and humanities, the books in the UTP Insights series contribute to public discourse and debate and provide a valuable resource for instructors and students.

BOOKS IN THE SERIES

- Paul T. Phillips, *Truth, Morality, and Meaning in History*
- Peter MacKinnon, *University Commons Divided: Exploring Debate and Dissent on Campus*
- Raisa B. Deber, *Treating Health Care: How the System Works and How It Could Work Better*
- Jim Freedman, *A Conviction in Question: The First Trial at the International Criminal Court*
- Christina D. Rosan and Hamil Pearsall, *Growing a Sustainable City? The Question of Urban Agriculture*
- John Joe Schlichtman, Jason Patch, and Marc Lamont Hill, *Gentrifier*
- Robert Chernomas and Ian Hudson, *Economics in the Twenty-First Century: A Critical Perspective*
- Stephen M. Saideman, *Adapting in the Dust: Lessons Learned from Canada's War in Afghanistan*
- Michael R. Marrus, *Lessons of the Holocaust*
- Roland Paris and Taylor Owen (eds.), *The World Won't Wait: Why Canada Needs to Rethink Its International Policies*
- Bessma Momani, *Arab Dawn: Arab Youth and the Demographic Dividend They Will Bring*
- William Watson, *The Inequality Trap: Fighting Capitalism Instead of Poverty*
- Phil Ryan, *After the New Atheist Debate*
- Paul Evans, *Engaging China: Myth, Aspiration, and Strategy in Canadian Policy from Trudeau to Harper*

TRUTH, MORALITY, AND MEANING IN HISTORY

Paul T. Phillips

UNIVERSITY OF TORONTO PRESS
Toronto   Buffalo   London

© University of Toronto Press 2019
Toronto Buffalo London
utorontopress.com

ISBN 978-1-4875-0453-3 (cloth) ISBN 978-1-4875-2338-1 (paper)

Library and Archives Canada Cataloguing in Publication

Phillips, Paul T., 1942–, author
Truth, morality, and meaning in history / Paul T. Phillips.

(UTP insights)
Includes bibliographical references and index.
ISBN 978-1-4875-0453-3 (hardcover) ISBN 978-1-4875-2338-1 (softcover)

1. History – Philosophy. 2. Historiography. I. Title. II. Series: UTP insights

D16.8.P55 2019   901   C2018-905730-0

University of Toronto Press acknowledges the financial assistance to its publishing program of the Canada Council for the Arts and the Ontario Arts Council, an agency of the Government of Ontario.

  Canada Council   Conseil des Arts
for the Arts   du Canada

 ONTARIO ARTS COUNCIL
CONSEIL DES ARTS DE L'ONTARIO
an Ontario government agency
un organisme du gouvernement de l'Ontario

Funded by the   Financé par le
Government   gouvernement
of Canada   du Canada | Canadä

For Paul, Maria, Jacqueline, Joseph, Callum, Thomas, Owen, Connor, Charlotte, and Grace, and to the memory of Brian Bond and Bernie O'Rourke

Contents

Preface ix

Introduction 3

1 Truth 19

2 Morality 40

3 Meaning 62

4 History beyond the Academy 105

Conclusion 127

Notes 135

Index 147

Preface

It is not uncommon for academic historians, if they are still in a writing mood at my age, to attempt to produce three types of works. One is the memoir – usually by the famous. I am not famous. And such books often have the power to offend. Given the recent debate over the accuracy of memory, there is yet another reason for publishers to discourage such submissions.

The second type of work is fiction, especially historical fiction, with its greater potential for financial gain for both writer and publisher. I have no expertise in this area. Like the memoir, it has the potential to offend anyone perceived to be the living model for some dubious character. In the case of both the memoir and fiction, one is well advised to publish and then leave town. I have no desire to leave town.

The third type of work is a sweeping narrative of world history, as attempted by the (fictional) retired historian in Penelope Lively's *Moon Tiger*. This is certainly not my intention. What I am attempting in this extended essay is to draw attention to three broad areas that, in my view, have received insufficient attention in recent years. My intended audience is the historian, both inside and outside academia, and any reader with an enthusiasm for history. Those in religious studies and philosophy with an interest in these questions might also consider reading what follows. It is not intended primarily for specialists in such areas as historiography, and, as a writer facing a similar situation recently said, I ask for some slack from them in these matters.

A great stimulus for this undertaking was not only the time for some stocktaking, as G.R. Elton would call it, in retirement but my work when called back as Gatto Chair of Christian Studies at St. Francis Xavier University in 2014–15. The subsequent two interdisciplinary seminars, especially the one dedicated to the theme of morality and history, and my public lectures, exposed me to many viewpoints. For this experience I am truly grateful.

I wish to thank John Blackwell, director, Research Grants Office, St. Francis Xavier University, for his unwavering interest in this project and Richard Isnor, associate vice-president, Research and Graduate Studies, at the same institution for his support at a crucial time in the completion of this manuscript. Margo Boyd, my administrative assistant, must be credited for her excellent work in the typing and preparation of the manuscript. Among faculty colleagues, I wish to thank Professor Laurie Stanley-Blackwell for her constant encouragement as well as Professor Sam Kalman, both of the History Department, and a host of other faculty members, especially in the St. FX Philosophy Department. At the University of Toronto Press, my thanks goes to Len Husband, my editor; Frances Mundy and Barbara Tessman; as well as the academic readers, for their expert advice and guidance.

Lastly, as with all my books, I thank my wife, Barbara, for her careful and critical reading of my manuscript and her advice regarding publication.

TRUTH, MORALITY, AND MEANING IN HISTORY

Introduction

> It [history] requires us to join the study of the dead and of the living.
> Marc Bloch, *The Historian's Craft*

The ancient Greeks had a great interest in themselves. Within this interest was a curiosity concerning their origins – in other words, how they got to where they were. This era is often seen as the birth of history in the Western world, exemplified in their great historians Herodotus and Thucydides. Yet we know that there were clear differences among these giants and the other early historians that followed in the Greco-Roman world concerning the scope and nature of what constituted history: so it has been and will probably always be.

History is based on the reconstruction of the past lives of human beings, the most complex of all creatures, and it raises many questions. What exactly caused a chain of events of great importance in the past? What are our sources and can they be trusted? Can we be sure that what we have uncovered truly explains what happened? What was the role of chance, or pure accident, in our search for causes? Do we understand fully all of the effects of the past? Can we know what was in the hearts and minds of those who performed specific actions, especially if, in our eyes, the consequences of those actions were evil? Are there patterns of behaviour that recur? Is there a meaning to individual lives or the lived lives of the human race collectively? Are we connected to other forces beyond us – be they gods or forces of nature – that guide our actions?

This book is concerned with most of these questions as well as some additional ones. It is grouped into three central areas of investigation, with chapters on truth, morality, and meaning. These areas do not function as sealed compartments, as there is much flow in the discussion from one to another. In relation to the first area, the older debate about accuracy in the reconstruction of the past has been joined by new perspectives derived from other disciplines and the media. Whether moral issues, especially moral judgment, are within the domain of historians is a constantly recurring debate. Meaning in history, or the lack thereof, has continued to be an interest for a minority in the academic profession, and perhaps for more outside it. In the view of the author, there is an urgency to discuss these areas. It is up to the reader to decide whether or not this urgency is real.

Now, if I shift to myself for a moment as a sort of case study, I shall raise some of the central questions in this book with reference to a life of over seventy years (don't worry – this is not an autobiography). How, for example, did I become a historian? From the time I was a schoolboy, I was always interested in history. Where that interest came from, I have no idea. Neither of my parents had any proclivity for it, nor did anyone else I can think of in my family. There were other subjects in school that caught my attention, and frequently I got better marks for my efforts there than in history. However, when I read outside class, which was not that often, it would be in history or historical fiction. The same was true of my choices in cinema.

As an undergraduate, my subject of concentration came to be history, by a somewhat circuitous route. Although my plan was to become a lawyer, my marks in history steadily improved. In my senior year, I decided to go on to graduate school, rather than law school, at least for the time being. I never left the profession once I entered it, but, facing some challenges, I often wondered if I had taken the right fork in the road.

In terms of my specialties in history, I can see more clearly some causes for the choices that I made. As my father was a European immigrant, taking the path of British and European history was probably based on interest in my roots. My dynamic mentor in graduate school was in social history, with a special interest in the roles of religions, and I soon was zealously consumed in study of the same interests in modern history. Both my parents were religious, although their traditions differed from each other. This probably explains both my early interest in the effects of sectarian strife and, as my own life evolved, other questions involving secularization and the challenges of unbelief. I can also see the causes of my later career pattern reinforced by professional rewards and advancement. However, looking back over my whole life, it could easily have gone in other directions. I am a fairly religious person (Catholic Christian), but I never felt much of a hand from above concerning my career – although in the other aspects of my life, there may have been times when I did. In defence of this thumbnail sketch of my life, I would invoke the name of the great historian E.H. Carr, who advises us that, in order to best understand what a historian has written, the reader should know something about the historian.

Further, in the interests of full disclosure, I would say that, in the fashion of most historians trained in my generation, I have tried to present the various sides of the central issues contested in this book in a spirit of critical inquiry. However, more than in any of my previous books, I have supplied and at times argued the Christian position. I have not attempted to present things in the "concealed mode of Christian apologetic," as Michael Bentley has said of Herbert Butterfield.[1] I do so openly.

As my mother advised me, being able to adapt to change is an essential part of any successful life, for life is about change. So too is it for those interested in the study of the past. History is largely about the lives of the deceased, whose active agency has ceased. However, as we search for the best ways of understanding the lives of the dead, our quest for approaches and techniques to accomplish this goal is itself unceasing and ever-changing.

While curiosity about our ancestors is as old as the hills, so too are distortions in what has been bequeathed to us concerning their lives. Some of these distortions were accidental flaws inherent in the mode of communication – especially in the oral tradition, which was used by the bulk of ordinary persons, who were illiterate. Written records, even those pertaining to the masses, tended to be produced by elites in societies for their own purposes. Histories produced in ancient times were often of an official nature, designed to praise the accomplishments of past rulers as well as to spread a sense of continuing loyalty, or perpetuate a sense of terror, in the public. They were often linked to religions supportive of the hierarchies in power, with mutually sanctioned penalties for non-supporters in this life and in the next. With such works heavily laced with self-serving mythology, it is anyone's guess as to how many people in these past societies felt these histories were credible. For example, most historians used to think that belief in the supernatural was true of almost all ancient civilizations. However, Tim Whitmarsh of Cambridge has recently raised some doubts about this, in the classical world at least, in his book *Battling the Gods* (2015).

As time passed, particularly in the Western world, demand arose for more accurate accounts of the past for more diverse tastes. Initially cohabitating the reading space of official narratives of state and church, the new approach gradually moved ahead. Since the Renaissance and Reformation, tensions between the two forms escalated, exacerbated by politico-religious warfare and the demands of a rapidly expanding reading public. And, not only the demands of competing religions and states but the Scientific Revolution and the Enlightenment encouraged fresh narratives designed to reinforce versions of progress other than the traditional one of Christian thinkers that ended in ultimate union with God.

Into this milieu appeared new waves of historians often linked to philosophy. Indeed, a branch of philosophy arose in the late modern period of European history, engaging those who sought meaning in history, among other things. Also, within the ranks of historians, the field of historiography was born (with historians, rather than philosophers, talking about history). Sometimes great events inspired the writing of history either in favour of or against these events and movements – the French Revolution is but one example – with writers often employing history as a tool in their arguments. And as literacy continued to grow, societies demanded more self-definitions of nationhood and greater numbers of people recognized the sheer pleasure in reading of the great adventures of the past.

Among philosophers, Georg W.F. Hegel (1770–1831) was the most influential in terms of history, with his idea of *weltgeist* – revealing the world spirit through history. He joined the mind to the material world, thus providing a mechanism that governed history and that was subsequently interpreted by a host of historian-philosophers in a variety of ways.

Michael Bentley has contrasted "the Enlightenment mode of historical thinking in France and Britain with a Counter-Enlightenment persuasion in the German-speaking world," arguing that these became the "twin poles of argument." Separated by these poles, "clusters of historiography" developed after 1800, the Enlightenment mode influencing those who favoured history as a social science (e.g., Auguste Comte, Hippolyte Taine, and Henry Thomas Buckle) from those who wanted an autonomy for history in analysis and explanation (e.g., Thomas Babington Macaulay, Thomas Carlyle, and Jules Michelet). For Bentley, German historian Leopold von Ranke held no "allegiance" to either position, although even he was unable to avoid the influence of Hegel's notion of *weltgeist*, much as he "hated it."[2]

Going beyond the German academic classifications of natural sciences and social sciences, history developed as a discipline of its own in Europe and North America in the late nineteenth century. When it had been taught earlier than this in the realm of higher education, it had often been linked to other subjects – in the English-speaking world, frequently with literature. As far as formal designations went, a century before the appearance of history chairs in western Europe, Britain had established Regius Professorships in History at both Oxford and Cambridge in the early eighteenth century. But these professorships were normally used as short-term political patronage appointments with no specific duties. As late as the mid-nineteenth century, Regius Professors were, as often as not, known more for their non-historical writings. "The dons," fellows of the colleges, did what teaching there was, including presumably some history.

Goldwin Smith, Regius Professor of Modern History at Oxford (1858–66), was unusually conscientious in his role, working closely with the dons in the teaching of history. But even Smith believed that philosophy held the "key" to history and must continuously inform the discipline.[3] He rejected the dominant historical thinking, instead strongly advocating moral judgments. He went on to be the founding professor of history at Cornell and a great influence upon the inception of the History Department at the University of Toronto, the city in which he resided for his later life. At Oxford, the research ideal, and the School of History, had to wait for his successor, William Stubbs.

By the early nineteenth century, chairs attached to actual schools of history, or at least the active teaching of history, had been established at German universities at Berlin, Göttingen, Leipzig, Munich, Kiel, and Jena. France lagged behind, with only two chairs, at the Sorbonne, as late as 1878. American, along with some British, students flocked to Germany, especially for graduate training in history. As we shall see in Chapter 1, Ranke's ideas of research in his seminar at Berlin became the gold standard for most professional historians.

By the 1880s, departments of history imbued with the research ideal began to appear in the English-speaking world. In the United States, Columbia and Cornell established proper departments of history in this period, and soon Germany ceased to be the finishing school of American students of history. In Canada, although chairs linked with departments had appeared at McGill and the University of Toronto, many students continued to go to Oxford and Cambridge for graduate study until the Second World War, probably a result of continuing imperial ties. Thereafter, for practical reasons, they went either to American universities like Harvard or to the established Canadian schools. According to Bentley, by 1900, American universities were turning out 200 PhD's in history each year. The undergraduate honours school at Oxford in the same period produced 100 graduates per year, and over 1,000 registered in history at the Sorbonne.[4]

In the United Kingdom, where PhD (or DPhil) training was not based on the rigorous German model, but rather focused on research theses, there continued to be a number of highly placed historians in academe without formal doctoral or even graduate degrees. With the proliferation of new universities after 1945, PhD's began to be the rule, including at Oxbridge. In Canada, where several highly placed academics continued to be trained at Oxbridge, some very esteemed academics, including Donald Creighton, did not possess a doctoral degree, even as late as the 1970s. However, some PhD's were produced at home, and others were recruited from outside the country to teach at Canadian universities. By the late 1960s, the academic historians flowing from the United States into Canada all possessed the PhD or were on the way to obtaining one.

Ultimately, as James M. Banner has stated, the research university came to be "the principal location of historical scholarship," through its "near monopoly over the accreditation of trained people in most fields of professional and intellectual endeavor, including history."[5] As he notes, "Without a doctorate ... – without certification that one has completed a course of study recognized as complete and legitimate by similar institutions and by peers in the same discipline – professional status is not assured and professional positions are hard to come by."[6]

R.I. Moore describes the period up to the 1960s:

> The parameters of the undergraduate curriculum, and of much of the greater part of research as well, were very largely those which had been shaped by Ranke and his pupils for continental Europe, and by Stubbs and his followers at Oxford, and through Oxford the British Empire. The agreement of the two traditions on the essentials of content if not always of method was variously but effectively demonstrated in North America.[7]

In the period roughly between 1880 and 1960, university departments of history gained full control over the training of professional historians – at least for those intending to be teachers or professors. In North America, a regimen of courses ascending from the general to the particular in scope became the order of the day. A compulsory Western civilization became somewhat of a norm at the first-year level, with increasing specialization and choice thereafter, usually entailing different nation states and restrictive time frames, culminating in senior year courses that might have a narrower focus or theme. Thus, it was virtually impossible for undergraduates majoring in history to not have exposure to areas beyond their final choice of country and period. This system became less rigid by the 1970s, with the expansion of curriculum into all areas of the world, and a multiplicity of choices are now possible. Towards the end of the twentieth century, global or world history began to challenge Western civilization as the compulsory first-year offering.

In Britain and other countries of western Europe, a variety of curriculum designs could be found. For example, at the more elite universities in England, the tutorial or seminar system prevailed, with closer interaction between academics and their students in the area of discussion and writing from first year onward. Especially in North America, little effort was made to incorporate secondary school subjects and approaches into the curriculum. This was curious, given that large number of history graduates took up teaching positions in high schools. History was always considered to be a "teachable" in the certification of teachers and could form a good qualification for other subjects, such as "civics" or "social studies" or, indeed, anything emphasizing writing skills.

Beyond teaching, a history degree on both sides of the Atlantic was considered to be a good background for those considering law, the civil service, the church, the armed forces, or a host of positions in the private sector. Promoting analytical thinking, organizational skills, and clarity in oral and written presentation, history seemed a good, no-nonsense sort of background. It was also a safe choice for those who were unsure about their futures after obtaining an undergraduate degree.

By the dawn of the 1960s, the postwar baby boomers were beginning to reach secondary school, and the demand for teachers rose steadily. This put pressure on universities to produce more teachers. Whether for the training of more teachers or the needs of a host of expanding professions, it was obvious that the supply of university instructors would also have to be increased.

Most leading universities required a PhD as the admission ticket to their faculties. Soon this would be the case for even the smallest of undergraduate liberal arts colleges. Although graduate schools did increase their output, this was often and inevitably accompanied by debates about the quality of the increased number of graduates. However, given the good reputation of most university historians, especially those supervising PhD theses, this caution seemed to benefit history departments.

The discussions about the production of PhD's were also complicated by other factors, such as the proliferation of new fields of research. Many older historians, who tended to view legitimate research as confined to constitutional and high political matters, looked with suspicion on the emerging field of social history. Soon many more areas of study would appear, including working-class history, black history, and women's history, and a host of other areas. In the case of the United States, the links to the movements for civil rights and women's rights and protests against the Vietnam War were obvious. Given these links, strife entered meetings of the American Historical Association and the Organization of American Historians. In Britain, old Marxists were joined by new Marxists, leading ultimately to the formation of such bodies as the History Workshop.

The demand for more voices to be heard was bound to come, even without politicization. After the publication of E.P. Thompson's *The Making of the English Working Class* in 1963, it was impossible, regardless of one's social or political attitudes, not to acknowledge that huge areas of history had been neglected. Sensitivity would increase the need to explore the world of the dispossessed, from the working classes and women to the Third World inhabitants so often victims of colonialism and imperialism. Thompson's idea, when fully applied, was to treat such groups as more than simply victims, to view things from their perspective. This approach was enriching and expansive, and, with the appearance of new tools such as computers to assist quantification, there was ultimately an explosion of research activity. It was a renaissance of historical activity.

However, fragmentation was an inevitable by-product, making cohesion in programs difficult to maintain. In time, the intense research activity would result in the proliferation of courses reflecting the enthusiasm of professors for their research activities more than a careful canvassing of what students wanted. Student ratings of professors appeared in this period. But, while useful in improving teaching styles, they tended to reflect reactions to the personalities of instructors. James Banner offers some especially wise advice to professors too bound up in the new areas of research: "Following one's interests ought to include a certain wariness about historiographical, ideological, and epistemological trends and even to lively lines of inquiry that, as experience has often proved, may soon wear themselves out and, giving way to new ones, leave historians who have hitched their careers to them professionally high and dry."[8] We have all known colleagues who repackaged themselves in terms of their new and current interests as a result of non-publication of the results of research in their older interests.

While I have presented a picture of a steadily expanding discipline open to new vistas of insight into the past certain, entrenched attitudes actually became re-entrenched. The wall of separation between history and the philosophers of history remained. E.H. Carr illustrates this point in his very influential *What Is History?* from the early 1960s:

> Writers like Berdyaev, Niebuhr, and Maritain purport to maintain the autonomous status of history, but insist that the end or goal of history lies outside history. Personally I find it hard to reconcile the integrity of history with belief in some super-historical force on which its meaning and significance depend – whether that force be the God of a Chosen People, a Christian God, the Hidden Hand of the deist, or Hegel's World Spirit.[9]

While historians in bodies such as the American Historical Association, in the tradition of earlier, endless discussions about objectivity, indulged in heated debate about the impact of outside ideologies on the profession, there was little challenge to this even more fundamental assumption voiced by Carr.

Also withering was the old tradition of seeing history books as works of literature. As Peter Novick has observed, "If the distinction between history and philosophy of history had been basic to historians, the most sacred boundary of all was that between history and fiction."[10] Gone were the days when due regard was given to the historical atmosphere and imagination conjured up by writers such as Sir Walter Scott. This mentality of "fortress history" separated the academy from the wider world of history as well as leaving the specific consideration of truth, morality, and meaning at the wayside, not enlivened by interaction with other areas, principally in the humanities. It increased historians' association with social science, which was also driven by concerns for funding. Beginning in the 1970s, these attitudes coincided with the practical problems faced by the academic discipline.

The boom in expanding numbers of history students and professors hit the first wave of a "bust" in the late 1970s and 1980s. It was principally the result of the end of the baby boom that resulted in diminished university enrolments by the 1980s. In turn, this meant a dramatic reversal in what had been expanding departments of history and prospects for newly minted PhD's. As Peter Novick has stated, with respect to US universities:

> In the mid-sixties fewer than 10 percent of history Ph.D.'s were looking for a job when they received the degree; by the late seventies and early eighties, more than one-third were still looking at graduation time. And the jobs that were available were often not all that attractive, many being temporary or part-time positions, as cautious or budget-conscious administrators were reluctant to make long-term commitments.[11]

In Canada, the pattern was slightly different. With, initially, a smaller percentage of young people at university, a continued cultural link to the United Kingdom (at least Oxbridge), and such close proximity to the United States, the growth of indigenous graduate programs seem to be in slow motion for a time. In 1945, small doctoral programs were largely confined to McGill and Toronto. But the expansion of old universities and the wave of new universities being built as well as the enthusiastic support for more Canadian history changed matters in the 1960s. Canadian nationalism also asserted itself in attempts to stem the constant flow of American and British PhD's into history departments in Canada.

By 1974, twenty Canadian universities had PhD programs in history – thirteen developing after 1960. Of the 534 history PhD theses in progress in that year, only 296 were in Canadian history. This ultimately meant that many positions specializing in non-Canadian history could be stocked by PhD's produced in Canada. However, the increasing numbers also had a downside, and the Canadian Historical Association called for a general cutback in the number of graduate students, an action similar to that taken by the American Historical Association five years earlier.[12]

The glut of history PhD's was made worse by the legal raising of retirement age in the United States and, subsequently, its removal in many places, including Canada, where working past sixty-five came to be viewed as a human right. Unfortunately, it meant increasingly diminished prospects for employment for those entering the ranks of university teachers, as professors chose to stay on until retirement suited their personal needs. Replacement positions became complex planning issues.

Department heads and higher administrators at universities and colleges took the opportunity to exact what they believed to be higher standards for those applying for positions, obtaining tenure and promotions, and even holding their positions. Student ratings were important, even if not always deemed reliable. Research productivity became the gold standard, even in small, undergraduate liberal arts colleges. This encouraged a culture of competitiveness in terms of output and the obtaining of research funding. Science came to be the model, to some degree, especially in the focus on the securing of funding as a criterion of success. And specialization and thinking of history as a science, albeit a social science, seemed to be the best way of obtaining funding. It also encouraged university historians to keep their noses to the grindstone. There was no practical encouragement for those interested in broader, somewhat abstract issues such as meaning, morality, or truth in history. Historiography courses dealt primarily with very current issues such as postmodernism and research tools.

History enrolments at universities recovered somewhat by the end of the twentieth century but never returned to the levels of the 1960s or to the percentage of history majors among general enrolments at universities before that. In very recent years, the situation has worsened again. Certainly some of the explanation for this must be found in the general perception that arts subjects will not help a student get a job after graduation. This message has been reinforced by the uncertain economic climate in the world since the recession of 2008. In a *Los Angeles Times* op-ed piece titled "History Isn't a 'Useless Major,'" James Grossman stated that the core humanities disciplines in the United States contributed only 6.1 percent of all bachelor's degrees awarded in 2014. This was the lowest proportion since college data began being systematically reported in 1948. Since 2007, history majors declined from 2.2 per cent to 1.7 per cent of all undergraduate degrees. Grossman also noted that "the drop is most pronounced at large research universities and prestigious liberal arts colleges."[13] This latter point, I think, would mean that, at institutions where belief in the intrinsic value of history should be strongest, it was simply not holding up. Certainly these universities and colleges would be the primary conduits for the production of future scholars. They also have tended to serve the most affluent and those on scholarship, where one would find less concern over personal debt and less pressure to find immediate employment after graduation, compared with students at less prestigious institutions.

Certainly departments in many universities started to respond to the worsening situation by selling the merits of a history degree in preparation for other vocations than the traditional one of teaching. This promotion of history degrees, while always present, has become much more aggressive. So too is the attempt to reach more employment areas where the traditional skills of the historian might be supplemented by additional departmental program training, such as in the area of public history. There are new lines of thinking in liaising with that huge and growing world of history beyond the academy.

James Banner has encouraged the idea that even historians ensconced in academe must reach out to ever-wider audiences, whether through publishing or public speaking. Gone is the limited idea of reaching the public by such traditional ways as the Reith Lectures on the BBC in Britain or the Massey Lectures on the CBC in Canada. As he states, "Surely there is a place both for specialized academic discourse and for general historical prose – for both 'scientific' and artful writing – and the two kinds of expression can be employed by a single historian, who over an entire career will enjoy, and ought to seek, opportunities to write for many kinds of audiences."[14] And there are many imaginative ways to achieve this with other forms of media. Let us hope that such efforts are actually rewarded in rank and tenure decisions by university departments. Alas, there are still some instances where academic hierarchies have remained both somewhat pretentious and intransigent in such matters.

If the "fortress history" mentality has led to historians avoiding association with other subjects such as philosophy and literature, and has kept their work from popular audiences, it has also erected a barrier to the full consideration of the benefits of closer dialogue with religion. The carefully preserved wall of separation between the "secular" world of the historian and the "religious" world of scholars in religious studies and even religious leaders interested in history has prevented potentially valuable exchanges of knowledge. This has been the case since the inception of the discipline in relation to Christianity and Judaism but has created even further denials of opportunities in the newer area of global history in relation to religions such as Islam and Hinduism. As C.T. McIntire has pointed out, dichotomies such as history versus religion, temporal versus spiritual, reason versus faith that are implicit in the division lead to exclusion of valuable insights and better research on both sides. They misunderstand "religion as a way of life" and ways in which "history manifests religion and religion manifests history."[15]

Whether or not the examination of the issues of truth, morality, and meaning by academic historians in a concerted manner, drawing on the wisdom of other disciplines, would help the sagging enrolments in university departments is speculation. The answer is not crucial to the message in this book, although, given the current state of affairs, it would probably do them no harm. Rather, I believe such an examination is necessitated by the discipline itself – to fulfil the very purpose of its existence. The alternative would be to continue with things as they are, embodied in what I have called fortress history. This could well result in other disciplines doing the job that, in my view, was intended for history. It would not end well. As Isaiah Berlin once stated, "There exists only two good reasons for the demise of a discipline: one is that its central presuppositions ... are no longer accepted ... The other is that new disciplines have come to perform the work originally undertaken by the older study."[16] These considerations also raise the question of the relevance of history – discussed years ago by Theodore Hamerow in his *Reflections on History and Historians* (1987).

The four chapters that follow address fundamental concepts underlying these issues. Chapter1, "Truth," is divided into a number of subsections, with due regard in one to the important influence of Leopold von Ranke. Chapter 2, "Morality," is structured in a similar way, with a section on Lord Acton. Chapter 3 "Meaning," features sections on Arnold J. Toynbee, who, like Acton on morality, made a notable contribution to the search for meaning in history, and Yuval Noah Harari, who has recently renewed this area of discussion, as well as my proposal for a renewed theist approach. Chapter 4 attempts to relate these concerns to the wider world of history beyond academia. The conclusion provides a summary of the issues, with a few suggestions for how the status quo might be changed. Each chapter and the conclusion is followed by a short list of suggested readings.

Suggested Readings

Michael Bentley, *Modern Historiography: An Introduction* (London: Routledge, 1999)

Marc Bloch, *The Historian's Craft* (New York: Vintage Books, Random House, 1953)

Peter Burke, ed., *New Perspectives on Historical Writing* (University Park: Pennsylvania State University Press, 1991)

John Cannon, ed., *The Historian at Work* (London: George Allen and Unwin, 1980)

H.P.R. Finberg, *Approaches to History: A Symposium* (London: Routledge and Kegan Paul, 1962)

Mark T. Gilderhus, *History and Historians: A Historiographical Introduction*, 7th ed. (Upper Saddle River, NJ: Prentice-Hall, 2010)

Arthur Marwick, *The Nature of History*, 2nd ed. (London: Macmillan, 1981)

Jeremy D. Popkin, *From Herodotus to H-Net: The Story of Historiography* (New York: Oxford University Press, 2016)

Fritz Stern, ed., *The Varieties of History, from Voltaire to the Present* (Cleveland, OH: Meridian/World Publishing, 1956)

John Tosh, *The Pursuit of History: Aims, Methods and New Directions in the Study of History*, 5th ed. (London: Routledge, 2009) chapter one

Truth

The search for truth is often thoughtlessly praised; but it has something great in it only if the seeker has the sincere unconditional will for justice.
> Friedrich Nietzsche, *The Use and Abuse of History*

Each historical narrative renews a claim to truth.
> Michel-Rolph Trouillot, *Silencing the Past*

E.H. Carr, in his singularly important book *What Is History?*, made the clear point that absolute truth is a goal "not appropriate in the world of history," except for the "simplest kind of historical statement."[1] Carr probably speaks for all historians since the late nineteenth century in this matter. It could not be otherwise. Historians deal with the remnants of the past experience of human beings. Without the benefit of time-travel machines, we can only approximate what actually happened. At the same time, I am sure there is a consensus of opinion among historians that Voltaire was wrong in stating that history is simply a lie commonly agreed upon.

This opens the question made famous by Pilate in his exchange with Jesus – What is truth? The website of the British Broadcasting Corporation, for example, states that, in general usage, the word truth is used in five different ways. There is the aesthetic version, referring to something that is broadly believable; the moral, referring to the truth within ourselves, like an instinct; the spiritual, which is something that is held to be true in the context of faith and belief; the scientific, which is something known as a result of empirical evidence and verifiable by repeated experiments; and the historical, which is similar to the scientific, in the sense that it is based upon evidence, but it is not verifiable by standard scientific experimentation. Added to the latter might be truths derived by deductive reasoning or other means peculiar to the study of human beings by human beings.[2]

But truth has almost always been closely linked to other realms. Carr argues that truth "straddles the world of fact and the world of value," a dual characteristic of the concept, which is present in all European languages.[3] Terry Eagleton has pointed to the ancient English pledge word still used in some wedding services, "troth," which means both truth and faith.[4] St. Augustine and St. Thomas Aquinas both linked the concept to love, the source of all virtues. Beyond religion, "truth" also shares an emotional quality with other areas of thought, even for supporters of science, who, according to Stephen Hawking, see not only the investment of reason but also of passion in the pursuit of truth.

Thomas Kuhn, in his book the *Structure of Scientific Revolutions* (1962), discussed the notion of a paradigm shift in relation to scientific truth. Kuhn argued that science through the centuries reflected changes in models of the universe that saw newer theories emerge as orthodoxies, not because they were truer, but because the majority of established scientists decreed them as such.[5] A similar lack of an absolute sense of truth is conveyed by Jeremy Popkin, who, citing as an example the work of Lynn Hunt on the French Revolution, states, "There might not be any single criterion by which historical truth could be defined."[6]

As Popkin has also pointed out, all major historiographical debates at bottom involve questions of human nature and existence, such as free will, in the quest for truth.[7] In the case of scientists, most do not believe in free will. Neuroscience today more or less sees the brain's making automatic decisions as inherent in its composition.[8] Yet, according to the Abrahamic religions, free will is traditionally thought to be exercised in the choices made by individuals to follow or reject the path of truth. For Yuval Harari, a materialist historian, the historic spiritual journey made by truth seekers has always been "tragic." For example, it motivated the Lutheran Reformers, often with great personal suffering, to overthrow the rule of the Roman Catholic Church, only to end up imposing their own laws and structures for religion. Religion, for Harari, is about the maintenance of social order, not the quest for truth.[9]

Background

Before the Renaissance, it is doubtful that every listener and reader in the Western world accepted every fact asserted in the chronicles of the past. The Bible, of course, was a sacred narrative, preserved in Latin and Greek and backed by the full authority of church and state. It was part of an enforced belief system that suppressed unauthorized, vernacular translations such as that of the Lollards. During the Renaissance, with its interest in classical times, some relaxation of the enforcement of the authority of such sources was allowed among the wealthy elites of Italian cities. This explains how, for example, Lorenzo Valla was able to prove that the document of the Donation of Constantine to the Papacy was a forgery.

Monitoring and enforcement became increasingly difficult following the invention and proliferation of moveable type printing presses. This development facilitated the spread of Reformation materials, with a concomitant growth in the reading population. However, it did not completely sweep away the power of authorities to determine what was considered to be truth in history, be it religious or civil. In time, however, a freer atmosphere of interpretation and belief would prevail.

History also came to be an important tool in propaganda, validating claims of dynasties like the Tudors or the various sides of the wars of religion in the seventeenth century. The Scientific Revolution, the Enlightenment, and especially the American and French Revolutions, all employed history as a tool of legitimacy, with arguments on all sides.

Gotthold Lessing's pamphlet attacking the veracity of Pastor Johann Goeze's sermons in 1778 in Hamburg launched the metaphor of "Lessing's Ditch." In this action, Lessing gave much publicity to the concept that so-called historical truths could be challenged in sacred narratives as much as in any other text of any other subject. Lessing anticipated the work of David Strauss in *The Life of Christ* early in the next century and, later, the work of devout biblical scholars in Germany and England who were willing to apply better standards of historical research to scripture in what was called the Higher Criticism. A movement thus expanded from so-called freethinkers (an earlier version of agnostics and atheists) to men and woman of faith demanding accuracy in writing history, including of the religious sort. Freethinking rationalists were already producing general works of history, such as those by David Hume and Edward Gibbon, that became quite popular among the literate.

The pressure on men of faith, who remained the majority of historians, to produce better work continued to increase. Against the proponents of rationalism and revolution, especially during and after the French Revolution, circles of historians became associated with the Romantics in defence of the older traditions. This was especially true in the German states, where historians were inspired by the approach of the Italian Giambattista Vico (1688–1744). Vico insisted that historians must use concrete evidence in their narratives. He developed a theory of regular stages of unfolding history reaching back to ancient times, from the Age of the Gods, to the Age of the Heroes, to the Age of Man (the last bringing equality), before a stage of collapse, which he believed would come to all civilizations. However, his influence derived less from his theory than from his empirical-like approach using inductive reasoning. And his belief in the overall unobtrusive superintendence of Divine Providence allowed historians of faith to accept him as a figure to be emulated.

It was no accident that German historians, inspired by Romanticism and nationalism, saw the first chair of history established at Berlin in 1810 in the last phase of successful resistance to Revolutionary France. Two years later, Barthold Georg Niebuhr published the first volume of his *Römische Geschichte* (Roman history), which was a model of critical evaluation of sources for future generations of historians. The inspiration of *Principi di Scienza Nuova* by Vico was clearly evident in Niebuhr's sharp reaction to the ideas of material and linear progress found in the rationalist school of Hume and Gibbon.

Reverence for the past and the Burkian slow, evolutionary preference for change also appeared in the writings of English figures such as Samuel Taylor Coleridge, leading John Stuart Mill to later coin the phrase Germano-Coleridgeans. A direct conduit of communication between Germany and England could be found in figures such as Julius Hare (1795–1855), originally a member of the Apostles club while at Cambridge and later a country vicar. Hare, one of few German speakers in English university circles, made a concerted effort to Germanize English intellectual life with publications such as the series *Guesses at Truth* which began in 1827. The German Romantic school had further influence not only through the essays and aphorisms of this series, but also indirectly in Hare's encouragement of others.

The Rankean Revolution

There was nothing in Leopold von Ranke's background that would have suggested that he would become the most influential historian among his colleagues in Europe and North America by the time of his death in 1886. Born into a devout Lutheran family in 1795, he studied theology and philology at Leipzig University and was hired as a schoolteacher in Frankfurt in 1818. Producing his first history book in 1824, he was appointed to a professorship of history at Berlin University a year later. Hard work, as revealed in subsequent publications, led to his elevation to the chair of history in 1834, which he held until his retirement in 1871. By that time, his seminar at Berlin had gained the attention of historians in Europe and North America. He remained an active scholar until his death.

In spite of his long list of publications covering important areas in the history of five major European countries, in a grand narrative style, Ranke claimed nothing special about himself. He urged historians to write in the service of "universal" or world history, which in actuality reflected the idea of the commonality of European history, with a preference for Western or the Latin and Teutonic peoples. He was concerned with prominent individuals and events and the energy of great opposing principles in wars and revolutions while diminishing the abstract and any single explanations. He believed in the importance of freedom of action under the overall, but yet not understood, plan of God for humankind. Traces of the thoughts of Immanuel Kant and Johann Gottfried Herder could be discerned in his work.

Ranke's teaching that the historian must understand the past as people who lived in it did, and then be able to describe the past as it actually was to the reader in the present, ultimately became the standard approach for all historical research. As a teacher at the University of Berlin for almost fifty years, and through the example of his many publications, he founded the modern discipline of history. His empirical approach seemed to conform to the emerging scientific spirit and gathered the best and most practical ideas on writing the history of past centuries. As he humbly stated, "History has had assigned to it the task of judging the past, of instructing the present for the benefit of all ages to come. The present study does not assume such a high office; it wants to show only what happened," the last words conveying the essence of his famous phrase, "wie es eigentlich gewesen."[10]

The objectivity of historical truth, the priority of facts over concepts, the equivalent uniqueness of all historical events, and the centrality of politics were Ranke's canons. It was clear to his disciples, as they journeyed to the many newly opened archives, what they must do. Yet, while Ranke urged them to work in the service of truth, the accomplishment of this task was not straightforward. Beyond methodology, which was his main contribution, Ranke held strongly to pious religious beliefs and deference in politics. All ages were of equal value in God's eyes and thus must not be judged by later historians. Therefore, in his conservative, Romantic vision, whatever existed was divinely ordered.[11] Ranke thus denied any elaborate pattern to history beyond the immediate trends that could be discernible to mere mortals. He believed that only theology and history together could share the truths of heaven and earth.[12] However, as Wilson Coates and Hayden White have said, in denying any possible philosophy of history, Ranke adopted a position that itself constituted a philosophy of sorts.[13] As Arnold J. Toynbee said of Ranke, "When he says all he is trying to do is to state exactly what happened, I get rather impatient. He is absolutely innocent of the theory of knowledge, and I think he ought to have been more sophisticated philosophically."[14] Ranke certainly laid the foundation for the more modern schism between the philosophy of history (philosophers writing about history) and historiography (historians writing about history).

Ranke's conservatism was not embraced by all who approved of his methodology. Lord Acton, the leading exponent of the Rankean method in England, suffused his own writing with the liberal-rationalist idea of progress. He even suggested that Providence equals progress when viewing the unfolding of modern history.

For both conservatives and liberals, believers and non-believers, the Rankean revolution ushered in a new era marked by the conviction that truth could be found through the empirical approach of reconstructing the past largely by researching original primary materials in archives. This idea coincided with momentous practical possibilities for newly minted researchers. Where access to the archive had once been exceptional, in the nineteenth century most archives (chiefly state) were opened to scholars in much of western Europe. As Acton declared, "The long conspiracy against the knowledge of truth has been practically abandoned, and competing scholars all over the civilized world are taking advantage of the change."[15]

For his part, Acton, as Regius Professor of Modern History at Cambridge, directed contributors to *The Cambridge Modern History* (12 vols. 1902–10) to write as objectively as possible in the interests of truth, avoiding the assertion of opinion and the pursuit of causes. Just as the newly founded School of History at Cambridge proceeded in the service of this "progressive science," so did the School of History developed at Oxford under the direction of William Stubbs, who inspired a whole generation of students to work with original documents in their research. Stubbs idolized Ranke: "Leopold von Ranke is not only beyond all comparison the greatest historical scholar alive but one of the very greatest historians that ever lived."[16] Ranke was also placed upon a pedestal in the United States and praised as the father of modern history. A host of future heads of history departments in that country even made the journey to be trained by Ranke or one of his disciples in German universities. The American Historical Association and the new wave of professional journals regularly evoked him as their patron saint.

In the late nineteenth century, an almost fanatical belief in the attainment of historical truth, as against all forms of "charlatanism," led to a drive among university historians to maintain objectivity. As Peter Novick has written, "historical professionalization, then, provided the underpinning of an authority which the norm of objectivity sought."[17] Through the years, there were significant challenges to this orthodoxy, including by Charles Beard and Carl Becker in their presidential addresses to the American Historical Association in the early 1930s. For such historians, "Definitions of truth ... were always social. One generation or society's truth was not another's."[18] For Becker and Beard, "history existed for man, not man for history. The historian's social responsibility was to provide an account of the past appropriate to society's current needs."[19] Rankeans counter-attacked such views with determination, and, by the 1950s, Beard and Becker had few supporters.

This Rankean empirical base seemed to justify some, if not all, of the approaches of the pseudo-scientific theories of an earlier wave of positivist historians in England such as Henry T. Buckle (d. 1861). The term "positivist" became widely linked with the Rankeans. By the early twentieth century, J.B. Bury, as Regius Professor of Modern History at Oxford, could confidently claim that history was a science "no less and no more."[20]

There was somewhat of a pack mentality in this claim to truth and objectivity. As Jonathan Gorman, a philosopher of history, has said, "Objectivity is not warranted by general agreement."[21] And there were still academics who saw historians as first and foremost producers of great literature. George Wrong, in his inaugural address as first professor of history at the University of Toronto in 1895, while praising the new wave of primary document use in schools of history, could also admire the work of E.A. Freeman, "who never used an ancient manuscript in his life."[22]

As the twentieth century progressed, the sheer volume of archival evidence began to problematize the initial claims that definitive truth had been achieved in professional historical writing. Different types of archives began to open their doors, and historians began to expand the narrow parameters of what tended to be seen as worthy of investigation. Whereas the focus had once been political and diplomatic events, social history, to name but one field, began to be pursued, using its own sources. Such developments belied Acton's earlier claim that "nearly all the evidence that will ever appear is accessible now."[23] Alliances with other disciplines in the pursuit of "scientific" historical truth became problematic, sometimes resulting in assaults on the Rankean-based orthodoxy, as, for example, with the application of psychoanalysis to historical analysis.

In Europe, and especially in Germany after the First World War, what has been described as a crisis in historical theory took place. Already before the war, Wilhelm Dilthey (1833–1911) expressed scepticism about Rankeanism, asserting that history could be only a re-enactment through the imagination of the historian. After the war, Dilthey's ideas were joined with those of Ernest Troeltsch and Heinrich Richert that history was more about myth building (*willenschaft*) than science. Inspired by the Italian historian and philosopher Benedetto Croce (1866–1952), such ideas found expression in English in the subjectivist idealism of R.G. Collingwood in his famous work *The Idea of History* (1946). History, these proponents argued, was a construct of the past in the writer's mind. Thus, it was basically subjective.

At the very least, it was clear that historians applied a selective process in their collection of evidence. This point was eventually most forcefully made by E.H. Carr in *What Is History?* (1961) in his discussion of distinguishing "historical" facts from other facts of the past. Carr noted that it might still be possible to claim history as a science, as the principle of selectivity was the actual way of modern science, or at least social science.

At the time that Carr published his influential book, many historians still claimed that outright truth seeking was what history was all about. As Fritz Stern stated, "The historian's fundamental commitment is to truth as it has been for centuries."[24] And, as Stern suggests, the consideration regarding truth lay at the very foundations of the study of history, even before Ranke. From the study's very beginnings in classical times, it was asserted that the construction of any narrative must be free of untruths (Cicero) and from the corruption of pressures from "friends" (Polybius) to be of any value. As G.R. Elton has stated, "If we honestly think that the study of history is a proper pursuit for civilization, that it amounts to a sincere and intense search for the truth, then we must take seriously the task of maintaining this study and this search for future generations."[25]

Elton, who was a giant in the field of Tudor history, as well as generally at Cambridge, where he was Regius Professor of Modern History, spoke for many historians in the middle decades of the twentieth century in stating that "there is ... a very large body of agreed historical knowledge on which no dispute is possible, and though this body of knowledge may not by itself provide a very sophisticated interpretation of the past it is entirely indispensable to any study of it."[26] Elton acknowledged Carr's point that there were many ways in which historians involved themselves in their pursuit of truth in the area of interpretation. But the danger in Carr's view, according to Elton, was the underlying assumption that the historian becomes the "creator of history"[27] in building arguments and selecting relevant evidence. In the turbulent sixties, with contemporary causes attempting to use history as a tool, the staunchest defence of the primacy of seeking truth was made by Oscar Handlin, a professor of American history at Harvard. Handlin fully recognized that the presentation of the past would involve an interpretive role for the historian. As he stated, "History is not the past, any more than biology is life, or physics, matter. History is the distillation of evidence surviving from the past ... No one can relive the past: but everyone can seek truth in the record."[28] To quote Handlin again: "The use of history lies in its capacity for advancing the approach to truth. The historians' vocation depends on the minimal operational article of faith: Truth is absolute; it is as absolute as the world is real. It does not exist because individuals wish it, any more than the world exists for their convenience."[29] For Handlin, the existence or non-existence of reality lies more in the realm of the philosopher.

Handlin, especially in the turbulent decades of the late twentieth century, was also concerned with bending the truth in the service of a cause. In the 1960s and 1970s, it was perfectly understandable that historians, especially young ones, would want to be part of some of the great movements advancing the cause of equality, from women's rights to those of the gay community, an end to war, and so on. It would be only natural for some to try to use their skills as historians in aid of such noble goals. Moreover, as Michael Bentley has pointed out, "At some point between 1960 and 1975 in most countries of the West, history took a turn toward theory … They [historians] began a journey (still continuing) away from telling the 'truth' about 'the' past towards a view that there are infinitely many sorts of past to talk about and towards a deep scepticism about discerning the truth about most of them."[30] Even the relatively dormant field of imperial/colonial history was suddenly shaken to its roots by the publication of *Orientalism* by Edward Said in 1978. Not only did Said's book offer a critique of European views of Asiatic colonial societies, but he argued that these views reflected not simply a separate colonial narrative by Europeans but were firmly within the thinking of the dominant paradigm of post-Enlightenment progress. For some of the postcolonialists who followed Said, as Frederick Cooper has stated, "The goal has been no less than to overthrow the place of reason and progress as the beacons of humanity, insisting that the claims to universality that emerged from the Enlightenment occlude the way colonialism imposed not just its exploitative power but its ability to define the terms, democracy, liberalism, rationality."[31] Cooper criticizes not the postcolonialist belief that colonialism was clearly within the values and structures of Europe but, rather, its exaggeration. Offshoots of postcolonialism have included postcolonial feminism, which has been critical of the focus of feminism on the exploitative nature of women's experience in Europe and North America. Other counter-criticism has also emerged. As Peter Novick has said of Said, he "seemed to be trying to have it both ways by denying the existence of a 'real' Orient, and savaging Orientalists for misrepresenting it."[32]

Nonetheless, Said's work inspired other historians to look at the non-Western world in a new way, including by working with documents, and especially oral narratives, not produced by Western administrators, observers, or elites. From India, such ideas generated the Subaltern Studies Group by the 1980s. In 2000 Dipesh Chakrabarty, a former Group member, published *Provincializing Europe: Postcolonial Thought and Historical Difference*, which, among other things, pointed to empiricist and historicist thinking inspired by Ranke as imposing European concepts of research on the rest of the world without due regard to the views and approaches of historians from other cultures. Clearly, the same events of the past could be viewed in very different perspectives, making the seeking of truth that much more complicated.

The net result could be the writing of great works of historical scholarship that expand the parameters of existing history or, indeed, the creation of new and valid fields of study. But there could also be distortions of the past to create parallels or bridges to the present from the past in the service of a present-day cause. As Handlin cautions, "All too few scholars are conscious that in reducing truth to an instrument, even an instrument for doing good, they necessarily blunt its edge and expose themselves to the danger of its misuse. For, when truth ceases to be an end in itself and becomes but a means toward an end, it also becomes malleable and manageable and is in danger of losing its character – not necessarily, not inevitably, but seriously."[33] This risk is not new. Many years ago Herbert Butterfield wrote extensively of a major problem in British history whereby the ancestors of modern Liberals were made to look like heroes. The "Whig interpretation of history" has become a generic term for similar distortions by historians in other fields.

Practical Problems

Scientists try to bring what they study under general theories; philosophers seek to discern the general nature of things; historians endeavor to locate things in their contexts.

William Dray, "Philosophy and Historiography"

Inherent in the use of archival-type evidence is the recurring problem of selecting certain things and rejecting others, even in the pursuit of the most straightforward of theses, let alone for a "cause." This problem can be magnified when one journeys outside the archives to other sources, particularly if one is not careful.

Particularly fraught is in the reliance on memory, often in connection with oral sources. How reliable is memory – individually or collectively? Trial attorneys have always known that, the longer the passage of time, the easier is it to lay a good defence. A mistaken detail about the scene of some tragic event can be used to discredit seemingly valid testimony. But, then again, a defence lawyer's primary goal is not the attainment of the essence of a truth but simply the creation of a reasonable doubt. And time may also erode details of collective memory, as in the case of some recent prosecutions of Nazi-era war criminals: how significant the erosion is ultimately left to the jury and judge.

Historians, in investigating their sources, have obviously been interested in seeking the essence of truth in past events. But here again the use of memory, no matter how pure the intention of the testimony, can be problematic. One writer has described memory as the past rewritten in the direction of feeling. More direct in his appraisal is David Shields, who, in *Reality Hunger*, states that "anything processed by memory is fiction."[34] Such thinking has actually led some libraries to reclassify autobiographies and memoirs as fiction.

In addition, in the creation of any narrative, no matter how short, is the problem of self-serving statements. We have all had the experience of discussing past events with friends and relatives and being corrected on matters small and big. Small details seem innocent enough, and we are usually willing to make concessions there, unless we want to prove that we are not on the path to dementia. But big details, especially those not reflecting so favourably on ourselves, are far more difficult for us. The higher the stakes, the more difficult it is to admit memory errors. The causes of rifts in a family, the path to divorce, the estrangement of a sibling or a child – these usually involve selective memory or, more bluntly, the suppression of important details. Coping mechanisms can come into play. All of these factors contribute to the difficulty in getting a clear picture of a major dispute in a family, a dissolved partnership in business, and so on.

On a grander scale, examples range from past public ceremonies to details contributing to wars. How significant were individual details, such as the attitudes of members of cabinet towards each other, in the making of key decisions? For example, a 28 December 2105 broadcast of a documentary on the origins of ISIS on the American news network CNN featured much discussion of the origins of the decision by the George W. Bush administration to invade Iraq. In spite of an abundance of taped interviews with all of the principal players on the US side, both during the events and later, there remain problems concerning which groups supplied inaccurate information and who was most responsible for the final decisions made.

Methods of reporting events in the media have also changed. While the camera and microphone have allowed journalists to report from the scene since the Vietnam War, distortions can take place. For example, the angle of a shot can make a protest or support group, or some battle action, look bigger or smaller. This and other distortions can be the indirect work of "media consultants" used by political leaders "embedded" among reporters. And there has been an advance of advocacy journalism in recent years, departing at times quite boldly from the goal of impartiality found in the training of journalists fifty years ago.

Occasionally, since the 1960s, streaks of gold can appear, such as the disclosure of the Nixon tapes during the Watergate hearings. Politicians and their assistants would be far more careful today in their inspection of files for the sake of their historical legacies. Long gone are the days of politicians such as William Gladstone who, as a point of honour, would leave their papers unedited in the archives for the integrity of the historical record. It is ironic that in an age of such intrusive media and a vast proliferation of records of all sorts, we can get a better idea of the thinking of politicians in the late nineteenth century than today.

Two more points here deserve mention. First, despite my remarks at the beginning of the chapter about the need for time-travel machines, such apparatuses, if they existed, would be no guarantee that the truth about a past event could be reconstructed. To simply witness great events, or even a sequence of happenings leading to great events, such as the outbreak of the First or Second World War, is not the same as explaining them. The historian must be able to understand the mentality and the inner workings of the mind of the principal actors. Even as far back as the empiricist Lord Acton, this began to be appreciated. Perhaps this is why he became so concerned about the internal thoughts of the great figures of history, anticipating both Freud and the field of psycho-history.

Second, too much focus on causation can lead the historian into a type of determinism, leaving out other factors such as accident and contingency. This is where even the sceptical realist E.H. Carr has been criticized.

Although the critics of the Rankean notion of the pursuit of truth have generally prevailed in the discipline of history, and the generation of thinkers, such as G.R. Elton and Oscar Handlin, who insisted on the existence of a body of unchallengeable evidence, have now passed away, we must continue to consider the consequences of abandoning the pursuit of truth. It is dangerous to say that one person's truth, is not another's.

Postmodernism

Literary critic Terry Eagleton believes that, for postmodernists, there can be no certainties and that convictions are authoritarian.[35]

This absence of a core reality, or truth, is the opposite of most religious faith as well as science.

Postmodernism began to influence the discipline of history in the 1960s but its impact was not really significant in the English-speaking historical world until the late 1980s. It grew out of the linguistic studies of early pioneers such as the Swiss academic Ferdinand de Saussure. Eventually the movement called structuralism was born, with the work of figures such as Roland Barthes. The manipulative power of language, as discussed by Louis Althusser, was soon applied by Claude Lévi-Strauss to anthropology and history and more widely in the theory of communicative action as developed by the German Marxist Jürgen Habermas. By the 1980s, the movement that came to be known as poststructuralism asserted that the meanings of words were produced differentially and hierarchically, with no real standards that could be accepted as objective.

In the 1980s, the term "deconstruction" emerged, with the assertion that texts had no inherent meaning, with every reader potentially taking their meaning differently. In other words, the "text" has a dialectical relationship with its reader, which determines its meaning. Thereafter, postmodernism emerged. It challenged the founding assumptions of Western culture, viewing with suspicion all existing systems of thought as elitist and arguing for the equal merit of popular culture. The most influential writer within this philosophy of knowledge was Michel Foucault, who believed that the episteme of the age of modernity (1700–1960) must be dismantled by postmodernists.

The applications to history were profound. Postmodernists viewed all history writing as the product of earlier discourse. Historical sources were themselves seen as the product of earlier discourse in a particular time and place. Historical truth was therefore highly relative. Hostility soon broke out between those who applied postmodernism to history and those who remained traditional believers of truth in history. Even some of the "relativists" on the subject – that is, those who were neither traditionalists nor postmodernists – began to grow uneasy. Lawrence Stone at Princeton wrote in 1992 that, in his early education forty or fifty years earlier, "the crude positivism of the late nineteenth century" already held no sway and that "historical truth" was seen as "unattainable." When he examined documents, he assumed that they were "written by fallible human beings who made mistakes, asserted false claims, and had their own ideological agenda which guided their compilation and therefore should be scrutinized with care, taking into account authorial intent, the nature of the document, and the context in which it was written."[36] Given this methodology, Stone asserted that he and many of his fellow historians were not "the positivist troglodytes that we are often accused of being"[37] by postmodernists. Stone's major point about the postmodernists was not their emphasis on carefully handling documents, or "texts" as they called them, but in the extremes of their arguments that "reality is defined purely as language. This is because if there is nothing outside the text, then history as we have known it collapses altogether, and fact and fiction become indistinguishable from one another."[38]

Other areas of conflict have been raised by Richard Evans, in *In Defence of History* (1997), in particular with reference to Jacques Derrida's statement that "there is nothing outside of the text," which leads to a seeming denial of the truth or "reality" of the past. Friendly to postmodernism, Callum Brown believes that it is not an ideology and that postmodernists "are not calling the past a text – they are calling all representations of the past texts."[39] Brown hopes some reconciliation can take place, perhaps by recognizing areas that are not in conflict, such as the infusion of much history writing with moral concerns that are never verifiable, whether by empiricist or postmodernist.[40]

Where Do We Go from Here?

As Peter Novick has said of the contemporary American scene, "various 'postmodern' intellectual currents worked together to chip away at the philosophical foundations of the objectivist posture."[41] Postmodernism, whether fairly or not, has been taken by many historians to mean that attempted representations of reality as de facto truth are futile and that all narratives are vulnerable to the distortion of language. Certainly such ideas have seriously undermined the empirical approach to history since Ranke, if not the whole idea, going back to Vico, of a science-like history based on sound historical knowledge. While Arthur Marwick may have correctly argued that dissident historians, from Hayden White to Alun Munslow, have failed to make their case, the stakes remain high, especially with Margaret MacMillan's recent assertion that, in the modern age of secularism, history has replaced religion as the prime tool in the validation of essential truths (see further discussion in Chapter 4). At the same time, we have seen a growing awareness of the abuses of history in the service of ideologies. There has been an enormous increase not only in the amount of material housed in archives but in new categories of primary sources driven by new areas of study, from expanded, non-elitist cultural studies to women's history. Evidence has expanded beyond written materials to film and television tapes used for documentaries as well as feature films. Since Marshall McLuhan's writings, an appreciation has emerged concerning the power of these and newer forms of media to shape our attitudes and reception of information. George Orwell already gave us an extreme taste of this power in the Ministry of Truth in his *Nineteen Eighty-Four* (1948). Attempts at objectivity have been replaced by advocacy in television journalism, including the very reporting of "news," as well as subliminal messaging through the Internet. Since the publication of McLuhan's *Understanding Media* (1964), human perception through electronic communication itself has come under analysis in very fundamental ways. It can be argued that the changes have been as fundamental as those produced by the rise of mass print after Gutenberg.

Under these circumstances, can history be trusted to convey truth? Disparate groups claim that it can. For example, some Protestant evangelicals in the United States argue that their interpretations of history, which draw on all forms of media from books to the Internet, can be trusted. At the other end of the religious spectrum, New Atheists also confidently assert that science-based knowledge can be trusted as reality and truth, rejecting any compromise with postmodernists.

The real answer may lie in accepting an incremental path to truth with resting stations along the way. St. Paul described the path to truth in our lives using a metaphor of the process of growing up, when we abandon childish thinking for seeing things in a more mature way, albeit as in a mirror dimly, before presumably the ultimate face to face in the next life (1 Corinthians 13:12).

Whether or not there is a next life, considerations of other possible dimensions of consciousness could force us to examine other ways of knowing, including, as suggested in so many philosophies and religions, the intuitive – something we today might call the subconscious or the imagination. Recent progress in neuroscience, especially on the brain, may uncover more on such ways of knowing. In addition, there are the possibilities of comprehending truth in an emotional sense as the spirit of ages captured in past fiction, thus reaching out to those other definitions of truth on the BBC website referred to earlier. As Eliot's character Harry in *The Family Reunion* says, "What did not happen is as true as what did happen."[42] British psychotherapist and essayist Adam Phillips, in his book *Missing Out: In Praise of the Unlived Life* (2012), describes the common experience of people living lives of unfulfilled potential by constantly thinking of other path(s) that could have been followed with potentially better results. Of course, it is pointless unless there is reincarnation. But it is perhaps part of being human. As Yuval Harari says, it is imagination that set Homo sapiens apart from all other animals (see the discussion on Harari in Chapter 3). T.S. Eliot described this capacity best, in *Burnt Norton*:

> Down the passage which we did not take
> Towards the door we never opened
> Into the rose garden.[43]

Northrop Frye in his book on T.S. Eliot points out that nobody lives a life where there is no place for thoughts on what might have been.

In the last resolve, perhaps the continued pursuit of historical truth is the important thing here, rather than claims to have acquired it in the most absolute terms. As Paul Ricoeur has observed,

"Only the practice of history teaches one to follow the narrow path between a positivism seeking to eliminate the historian in the name of history already written in the documents, and an irrationalism concluding on the basis of the historian's intervention that history lacks objectivity or truth."[44] Seeking this narrow path might be the solution to retaining what is best about the empirical methodology since Ranke and respecting the valid criticism of it. As for what we gain from our research, it might include levels of truth from the very concrete to the poetic. Humanity can profit from both ends of the spectrum and everything between.

A carefully cultivated middle ground seems a reasonable and somewhat pragmatic solution to the problem. It would probably appeal to a majority of historians interested in, or even trying to avoid, the issue. A recent study, *Telling the Truth about History*, by Joyce Appleby, Lynn Hunt, and Margaret Jacob, would appear to have arrived at the same solution. But is this the answer? For an earlier generation of historians no longer with us (e.g., G.R. Elton, Oscar Handlin), it would probably not be enough to quench their thirst for truth. Notwithstanding the words of St. Paul about a mature view of the world seen through a mirror dimly, it would certainly not be enough for many Christians or for some people of other faiths, nor perhaps for New Atheists who argue their convictions with such determination. For most dedicated persons of science, as described by Hawking, pursuit of their subject involves passion. The emotions are involved no less in history, whether in the pursuit of truth or the exploration of the issues of morality and meaning, as we shall see in the next two chapters. To end the debate with a tilt towards relativism would be to diminish a very important dimension of the discussion.

Suggested Readings

Callum Brown, *Postmodernism for Historians* (Harlow, UK: Pearson Education, 2005)

E.H. Carr, *What Is History?* 2nd ed. (London: Penguin Books, 1987)

Dipesh Chakrabarty, *Provincializing Europe: Postcolonial Thought and Historical Difference* (Princeton, NJ: Princeton University Press, 2000)

Frederick Cooper, "Postcolonial Studies and the Study of History," in *Postcolonial Studies and Beyond*, edited by Ania Loomba, Suvir Kaul, Matti Bunzi, Antoinette Burton, and Jed Esty, 401–22 (Durham NC: Duke University Press, 2005)

Terry Eagleton, *Reason, Faith and Revolution: Reflections on the God Debate* (New Haven, CT: Yale University Press, 2009)

G.R. Elton, *The Practice of History*, 2nd ed. (Oxford: Blackwell, 2002)

Oscar Handlin, *Truth in History* (Cambridge, MA: Belknap Press of Harvard University Press, 1979)

Leonard Krieger, *Ranke and the Meaning of History* (Chicago: University of Chicago Press 1977)

Peter Novick, *That Noble Dream: The "Objectivity Question" and the American Historical Profession* (Cambridge: Cambridge University Press, 1988)

Leopold von Ranke, *The Theory and Practice of History* (Indianapolis: Bobbs-Merrill, 1973)

Paul Ricoeur, *The Contribution of French Historiography to the Theory of History* (Oxford: Clarendon Press, 1980)

Edward W. Said, *Orientalism* (New York: Vintage, 1978)

chapter two

Morality

The issue of moral behaviour is not limited to the realm of history. It is a central concern of both religious studies and philosophy. It also lies at the very foundations of the legal systems of most countries. It is less central to science, though in areas such as weaponry, genetic engineering, and the environment, and in many aspects of social science, moral issues can be highly relevant and vigorously debated. Curiously, today many, if not most, professional historians would argue that it has no place in the study of history. The purpose of this chapter is to explore the reasons for this situation and to foster some rethinking on this subject.

Background

First of all, it would be useful to clarify the term "moral judgment." E.H. Carr in *What Is History?* made the point that in shaking out "historical facts" from other facts in the past, we "presuppose some measure of interpretation; and historical interpretations always involve moral judgements – or, if you prefer a more neutral-sounding term, value judgements." As historians deal with movements in times past, Carr also indicated, they often use words of a similar nature such as "progressive" or "reactionary," rather than "good" or "bad." However, for most historians, "the emergence of a particular value or ideal at a given time and place is explained by historical conditions of place and time."[1] In all cases,

Carr believed that the historian is not there to judge the private lives of past figures as good or bad. With respect to public figures who had powerful roles to play, Carr quoted Croce that "men of the past who belong to the peace of the past and as such can only be subjects of history ... can suffer no other judgement than that which penetrates and understands the spirit of their work."[2] What they unleashed in history is a more complex question.

William Dray has made a number of further observations on the question of moral judgment. He notes that, for those who believe history is "inescapably value judgemental," there seem to be a number of factors at play. When historians select historical facts, Dray believes, like Carr, that they render a value judgment about what is "important" about something in the past. And, according to Dray, the importance of something is usually determined by measuring its consequences. In turn, in order to be meaningful, "consequential importance presupposes intrinsic importance." He makes the point that feminist revisionism, for example, has noted that more attention needs to be paid to the intrinsic importance of women – "what makes their activities and experiences important, and selectable, may not be less what they helped to produce than what they had to endure."[3]

Any discussion of morality in history must begin with some basic questions. What are the parameters of morals in terms of the individual and the collective? What is the source of the moral order? Is the moral system a constant for all ages and all peoples? Does the historian have a right, if not a duty, to make moral judgments about figures, institutions, and actions in the past? Or, to put the last question another way, is it necessary for the historian in the service of objectivity to remain neutral or without comment concerning what some would call "evil doing" in the past?

A.C. Grayling has written about the important distinction between ethics and morals. For this philosopher, ethics is "a far broader matter than the moral considerations it includes within it, it is about the achievement of intelligent human well-being and well-doing. Ethical reflection concerns what sort of people we should be." On the other hand, "Morality is about what is permissible and forbidden in particular realms of behavior; ethics is about one's character."[4]

Grayling goes on to state that "one's ethics is one's own responsibility; morality is the responsibility of a social conversation, a discussion, even a negotiation, which ethical individuals must engage in."[5] Though by no means satisfying everyone, it seems to me that Grayling's distinctions are useful for the time being. They could, for example, be another argument for excluding the private lives of individuals in history from moral judgments, as urged by E.H. Carr, making "ethics," as opposed to morality, beyond the historian's jurisdiction.[6]

Grayling, a secular humanist, does not believe that the origins of one's own ethical propensities or of our moral or "value" system lie in God. Rather, as he and many others see it, these systems arise out of our humanity. In contrast, for example, C.S. Lewis, a renowned apologist for Christianity in his famous book *Mere Christianity* (1952), saw a near-universal pattern of agreed upon good behaviour with its origins in God. Indeed, for Lewis in his description of how this pattern can be discovered in a casual fashion in everyday life, this near code of behaviour is proof of the existence of a Divine planter of such impulses. This code has sometimes been called natural law, a concept stretching back at least to medieval Catholicism, if not ultimately to the (retroactively baptized) Greek philosophers Plato and Aristotle.

Another root traces the Western precepts of moral behaviour back through early Christianity and ultimately to the Hebrew prophets by the path of Revealed Religion. As Northrop Frye has demonstrated in *The Great Code: The Bible and Literature* (1982), the Bible, in particular, powerfully influenced all forms of literature into modern times, including plot forms paralleling the narrative from the Fall of Man to redemption. These forms would include historians making statements of moral lessons in poetic or mythological ways outside the need for particular statements to be verified in fact. By the late eighteenth century, however, Enlightenment writers wrote histories demanding more verification, at least on those statements that were easily falsifiable. Comparative approaches to other religions also became a fashion. Added to moral lessons conveyed in secular histories were other values, such as those of liberal rationalism. Nineteenth-century writers imbued with such ideas and newer ones such as nationalism were apt to project back into earlier centuries such notions and were subsequently checked and caught, as we saw, at least for Britain in the twentieth century in Herbert Butterfield's classic work, *The Whig Interpretation of History* and its derivatives.

Nevertheless, value-laden writing was commonplace in the nineteenth century, with competing visions of what would be the best path for the future of nations, whether England, Germany, or others. The rousing of patriotism became commonplace. But so was the continuing production of moral statements. William Stubbs, for example, the founder of the rigorous archives-based research ultimately characteristic of the entire School of History at Oxford, was himself in that category. While arguing against making moral judgments a systemic affair, Stubbs made regular moral statements by way of lessons suitable for the training of the young men attending his lectures who would most likely end up being civil servants or clergymen. One historian suggests that Stubbs's particular stance within the Anglican fold was even clearly revealed in much of his scholarly work.[7]

Stubbs, like many academics of his day, was a clergyman himself, and such attitudes were to be expected. Free will, they thought, must be guided and informed in making choices. Such attitudes were of their time, a long way from the mid-twentieth century, when, as Christine Davies has argued, "causalism" or social consequence, rather than fixed Christian principles, would begin to inform laws and regulatory norms in the Western world.[8] These values were also evident in the writing and teaching of academics who were not clergy. A good case in point was Goldwin Smith, a historian-academic, who was, interestingly, deeply critical of the role of the clergy in higher education.

Born into an affluent family in Reading, England, Smith went to Eton, studied classics, and then went on to Oxford, ultimately obtaining a first class in Literae Humaniores, as well as an assortment of prizes in Latin and Greek at Magdalen College in 1845. The next year, Smith entered the ranks of teachers being elected for the Stowell Fellowship in Civil Law by University College. He succeeded A.P. Stanley in this position and so became identified with liberal theology. Within this Broad Church circle of the Church of England, Smith became a strong advocate of university reform, with the objective of ending clerical preferments, as well as changes in the curriculum, including the bolstering of science. His educational liberalism caught the attention of Whig liberal politicians in the wider world, and in due course he served on parliamentary commissions, ending with his appointment as Regius Professor of Modern History at Oxford in 1858.

Smith's tenure at Oxford was not lengthy, and it was even shorter at Cornell, where he migrated in 1868 before coming to Toronto. Although quite interested in the development of the University of Toronto, located in the city where he resided from 1871 until his death in 1910, he held no official appointment there. Living on his ample personal wealth and that of this wife, he much preferred the life of an independent scholar. His manifold contributions to the field of history continued until his death. His writings reveal a combination of mid-Victorian liberalism with some common racist and sexist attitudes of his day, including a high degree of anti-Semitism. Though predating the founding of the modern schools of history at Oxford and Cambridge, he was dedicated to the imparting of knowledge, including teaching, and he was deeply concerned with the relationship between his evolving beliefs in moral philosophy and the field of history.

Moral judgment was especially important to Smith. As he stated famously in a passage reproduced in the inaugural lecture of Lord Acton as Regius Professor at Cambridge, "A sound historical morality will sanction strong measures in evil times; selfish ambition, treachery, murder, perjury, it will never sanction in the worst of times, for these things are the things that make times evil – Justice has been justice, mercy has been mercy, honour has been honour, good faith has been good faith, truthfulness has been truthfulness from the beginning."[9] Smith exercised his moral judgment with respect to individuals, events, and institutions in history as vigorously as any historian of his time. In Toronto, he came to have much influence on George Wrong (1860–1948), founder of the University of Toronto History Department. In his own inaugural address, Wrong concurred with Smith's view of the obligation to render moral judgments in history, stating that "the world is old, not young, and human nature has through the centuries remained unchanged. Social conditions have been improved, manners have softened, we are more enlightened, but we have still the same old strength and weakness."[10]

Thus Smith and his protégé had concluded that the same moral standard may apply regardless of the time frame. Smith generally adhered to the virtues of the new archive-based approach to history but did not see it as the automatic path to truth. Smith believed in the continuum of past, present, and future actions under the umbrella of unchanging human nature. Similar to E.A. Freeman, he held race to be of great importance. Blurring distinctions between contemporary and past issues, he showed much in common with Sir John Seeley in seeing history as past politics and politics as present history. However, he also believed that more attention should be given to cultural factors and came to be a great fan of Sir Walter Scott. As a man of literature, he believed that understanding the emotional impulses of history was as important as the uncovering of facts.

What seemed increasingly to unsettle Smith was the origin and source of authority in making moral judgments in history. His evolution from liberal Anglicanism, through what he termed Rational Religion, to a position of agnosticism in *Guesses at the Riddle of Existence* (1897) made his moral philosophy an uncomfortable partner. He sensed that his essential moral judging role as a historian was being compromised. At the same time, his rejection of ethical humanism left him not only without any sort of yardstick but with no clear way to enter into the conversation about the negotiation necessary for the establishment of a moral system, as described by Grayling.

There were plenty of agnostics and atheists in the historical profession and elsewhere who did not paint themselves into a corner in the way that Smith had. Grayling himself, for example, has pointed to a generally agreed list of moral precepts. As he states, "There are objective facts about human needs and interests that constrain any possible morality."[11] Like Christian theologians, he conceded that there will be some degree of variation in cultures and periods of history but "there are common themes throughout."[12]

A few years earlier, Richard Dawkins in *The God Delusion* (2008) has argued that our morality was never grounded in the holy books of religion. In the section entitled "The Moral Zeitgeist," Dawkins boldly asserts that, with the exception of religious extremists, there has been a consensus that prevails "surprisingly widely" on what is right and wrong.[13] He has been joined by fellow New Atheist Sam Harris, a neurologist who, in *The Moral Landscape* (2010), predicts the development of a robust ethical/moral system that can be global and science based. Harris already sees a science of human well-being that is clearly framed and well expressed, rejecting the fuzziness of postmodernists. For Harris, moral relativism is unacceptable. The implications of these new arguments for the numerous historians still who reject moral judgments in history have yet to be fully considered.

Returning to those who began to form the majoritarian view among historians by the end of the nineteenth century, much again is claimed in the name of Ranke. In the world of history, especially in North America, he is remembered as the father of modern history, largely for his methodology. Almost mythological, it viewed moral judgments as compromising objectivity and as unprofessional. North American proponents of Ranke remember little about his approach beyond this.

It is true that Ranke's historicism (*historismus*) was the bottom line – he believed that people could be understood only in terms of their history and therefore not in the realm of philosophy. History, for Ranke, was about individuality and constant change. This view necessitates analyses of specific and concrete events. Ranke was by no means alone in this view, or in laying aside natural law. As Michael Bentley has pointed out "German historians reject the imposition of an ethical code from above the events and allow the events to announce their own morality."[14] At the same time, Ranke held conceptual views beyond his alleged scientific empiricism. He believe that God's influence, through the spiritual energy exhibited by the state, was present, but there simply was no proof of this influence in purely human terms. As Bentley notes, Ranke "places events under God's hand and sees in their tendency God's moving figure."[15] In practice, this disposition was of no particular importance to the practical day-to-day work of historians, but is important to note.

Lord Acton: The Historian as Moralist

Lord Acton (John Dalberg Acton, 1834–1902) was perhaps the greatest figure in nineteenth-century England in the transformation of the study of history into a professional, academic discipline stressing objective, rigorous research. And he is equally remembered, and frequently condemned, for being one of the strongest advocates of the exercise of moral judgment by the historian. The main purpose of this section is to attempt to understand how these positions, which many historians would consider almost contradictory, could have been held by this renowned public intellectual. Acton's life was a fascinating one, but I will concentrate on only those elements that may shed light on the central concerns of this chapter.

Born in Naples in 1834, John Acton was a descendant of an English Catholic gentry family that had served the Bourbon kings of the Kingdom of the Two Sicilies in Naples for two generations. His father died when John was very young, and the boy, an only child, was moved to France by his mother, who was descended from a German Catholic aristocratic family that had resided in France for a generation. Soon his mother married again, this time to Lord Grenville, a member of one of England's most powerful Whig-Liberal families. John was then moved to a succession of Catholic boys schools in England.

In his mid-teens, and showing signs of considerable intelligence and scholarship, John Acton was sent for a short time to Edinburgh by his stepfather to sharpen those qualities even further, with the plan to seek admission to Cambridge University. Cambridge, where his uncle, a Catholic cardinal, had studied, seemed a realizable goal, but recently its colleges had reverted to a more rigorous enforcement of the religious test of membership in the Church of England, and Acton experienced crushing rejections by no fewer than three Cambridge colleges because of his Roman Catholicism.

His stepfather, who was not Catholic, was equally disappointed, given the time and money he had invested in the boy and his hopes for his future. There seems to have been no possibility of compromise. His mother and teachers had laid a solid foundation of Catholicism in young Acton. As he himself would often express throughout his life, the Catholic Church and its sacraments were dearer to him than life itself.

Answering his fervent pleas for a higher education, his parents sent him to Germany to study under one of that country's most distinguished theologians and historians, Ignaz Dollinger (1799–1890). Upon Acton's arrival in Munich, Dollinger quickly recognized his great intellectual capabilities. He was also introduced to a circle of liberal Catholic intellectuals, for Dollinger was also a Roman Catholic priest.

Dollinger's approach to history was inspired by the movement headed by Ranke that applied the spirit of science, or *wissenschaft*, to the study of history. As we have seen in Chapter 1, for Ranke, the scientific approach included the pursuit of strict objectivity in discovering historical truth or, to put it his way, how things actually were. This approach emphasized the purity of seeking only facts unearthed through rigorous research in primary documents in archives. As Acton wrote years later in his inaugural lecture as Regius Professor of Modern History at Cambridge, "Ranke is the representative of the age which instituted the modern study of history. He taught it to be critical, to be colorless, and to be new. We meet him at every step, and he has done more for us than any other man."[16] But the Rankean way was primarily one of methodology. For most historians (including Ranke himself), it could not supply an overall meaning to history.

In the course of his years in Germany, Acton met Ranke many times, and they became great friends. Often accompanying Dollinger, Acton also visited archives and was trained in the use of primary sources, not only in German state archives but in Venice and, ultimately, some twenty European locations in later years. By then he had also perfected his linguistic skills, being fluent in five languages and with a reading knowledge of more.

Returning to England in his mid-twenties in 1857, he inherited the Acton ancestral estate of Aldenham with its ample income, refusing, it is said, all income from Italy after the repression of the Sicilians by their infamous King "Bomba" (Ferdinand II, 1820–59). By now a liberal in politics, as well as philosophically and within church circles, he was willing to become a member of Parliament in 1859, representing a largely Catholic constituency in Ireland through the patronage of his stepfather. But he had little interest in the activities of ordinary politics, rarely attending sessions of the House of Commons. Nonetheless, he had quickly captured the attention of the Liberal Party leadership – especially William Gladstone, who would be Victorian Britain's most famous and longest-serving prime minister. For services rendered as adviser and intellectual inspiration for a host of policy matters, he was awarded a hereditary peerage in 1869, thus becoming Lord Acton. He also devoted time and considerable money founding and editing a number of liberal Catholic journals, such as the *Rambler* and the *Home and Foreign Review*, as well as expanding his library at Aldenham to over 70,000 volumes – one of the largest personal libraries in Europe. Earlier, in 1865, he fulfilled the deathbed request of his mother to marry Countess Maria Arcon, a member of an aristocratic German Catholic family. In the process, he added to his holdings the small Arcon estate in Bavaria, a place he had regularly visited in his student days in Munich. Acton's marriage was at times a stormy one, but there was no doubt that he and his wife were devoted parents to their six children.

Acton took particular interest in raising his children in the Catholic faith, and it is the nature of that faith that I now wish to discuss, for I believe it is a key to understanding the man and his approach to history. As E.H. Carr advises, you must know the historian in order to fully understand his or her work. Acton's faith has sometimes been described as childlike when compared to that of figures such as Cardinal Newman. Unlike Newman and many other English Catholic intellectuals, he was not converted to Catholicism by some theological concept. He was born into his faith and was held in it by the most rudimentary and emotional attachments. He adhered firmly to the regular observance of the sacraments and to Catholic devotional practices, literally to his dying day. Speaking for himself, I think, as well as most Catholics, he once wrote that the spirit of Christianity came from the life of Jesus, and "to the millions that cannot read, that have no sense of metaphysics ... it has been everything."[17] Yet, while the sacraments strengthened the individual in the exercise of free will in choosing good over evil, in the face of original sin and the world, the flesh and the devil, they did not guarantee this choice. Moreover, such choices have been made by all human beings through the ages. Thus, as Acton stated, "The ethics of History cannot be denominational."[18]

Acton believed that we were not alone in this world. He embraced the belief, based on scripture, in the benevolent guidance of God in our individual lives and in the collective affairs of humanity. This belief in Divine Providence was widely held by Christians, no less so in the nineteenth century. In all of his narratives, William Stubbs, often seen as an exemplary apostle of the new methods of rigorous research as one of the founders of the School of History at Oxford, saw such providence as the agency by which moral authority more or less triumphed. Ranke saw it in the workings of some national histories and as the driving force in "universal" or world history. He believed that, in modern history, England spearheaded this advance until the mid-nineteenth century, and that it was possibly being replaced by Germany.[19] In this, Ranke tended to believe that Providence was at work justifying what was manifested in the political and social order of the day. Against this historicism, "Acton offered the alternative theory of Liberalism," pointing to what *should* be, "irrespective of what is."[20]

Rejecting these tendencies in Ranke as a presumptuous interpretation of God's will, Acton wrote, "There is not a more perilous or immoral habit than the sanctifying of success." "Almighty God is not always on the side of the majority," he noted, and "what succeeds in this world has not always the blessing of the next."[21] Indeed, he argued that Providence was more apt to be revealed in the continual extraction of good from evil, and in the way in which people could profit even from defeats and mistakes and in subjugation.[22]

Yet Acton did believe that "Providence means progress."[23] Building on the widely held Judeo-Christian concept of a journey towards the goal of ultimate union with God at the end of time, he stressed that humanity would experience many setbacks, including short and even quite long defeats at the hands of the evil forces – this is easily demonstrated in any impartial examination of history. Such setbacks were the price (a consequence) of free will. But it was also God's gift to us to know the difference between good and evil through a moral code that, "in its main lines, is not new." He believed that "the difference in moral insight between past and present is not very large."[24]

In expressing such views early on, Acton experienced almost immediate opposition. Dollinger thought he exhibited the rigidity of an angry young man. Acton countered that, in his sheltered life, Dollinger appeared to have no knowledge of wickedness. Later, in 1887, in a key exchange with Mandell Creighton (an Anglican), whom he viewed as morally lenient in not condemning the actions of medieval popes, Acton wrote, "The inflexible integrity of the moral code is, to me, the secret of the authority, the dignity, the utility of history. If we may debase the currency for the sake of genius or success … then history ceases to be a science, an arbiter of controversy, a guide of the wanderer, the upholder of that moral standard which the powers of the earth, and religion itself, tend constantly to depress."[25] The judicious exercise of the moral code by the historian is, therefore, the guarantee of truth and objectivity.

To this end, Acton supported liberalism because it promoted liberty. "Liberty," he wrote, "is the condition of duty, the guardian of conscience. It grows as conscience grows … So that liberty ends by being Free Will."[26] When asked, "What is the way of Providence?" He replied, "Towards, liberty, its security, conception, enjoyment."[27] Some later historians, such as Herbert Butterfield, have accused him of being Whiggish, in the fashion of Lord Thomas Babington Macaulay, of denying the autonomy of history through his admiration of recent achievements of the present. But Acton's view of progress was never so narrow. To ratify the present order of things was never his intention. And, in viewing the past, the defeat of good causes was always in his mind.

Acton coined the famous phrase "power tends to corrupt, and absolute power corrupts absolutely."[28] Rejecting the well-known great man theory of history associated with Thomas Carlyle, he also stated that "great men are almost always bad men."[29] To excuse evil actions as necessary on the grounds of rank and power was never acceptable.

Thus, a struggle was constantly in the mind of Acton between the corrupting aspects of power and freedom. As primarily an intellectual historian, he stressed ideas as the driving force of history and argued that the ideas driving history were more or less the same as those driving the present. In fact, he believed that modern history, his domain, covering the past four hundred to six hundred years, should be taught from this stance. But he was not so naive as to believe that even liberalism could be altogether trusted. As a Christian, he knew the workings of sin in this world. As he stated, "We contemplate our ideas in the sunlight of heaven and apply them in the darkness of earth."[30]

For Acton, religious liberty was the foundation of all the liberties, a lesson he had learned in his teen years as a member of the Catholic minority in England. It must include all other religions, for religious liberty is possible only where the co-existence of different religions is recognized, with an equal right to govern themselves according to their own principles. That is why the persecution of so-called heretics was wrong, whether instigated by popes or saints. He admired and defended the writer George Eliot (Mary Ann Evans) against her critics, and argued that she was very ethical, to the limits of her humanistic atheism. And within the Catholic Church as a liberal Catholic, which he defined as the quest for liberty within the church,[31] he rigorously and publicly opposed the doctrine of papal infallibility, never receiving the excommunication that befell Dollinger.

Much has been said of his estrangement from the Catholic Church in the 1870s and 1880s, with some arguing that it forced a silence in his writing following the promulgation of papal infallibility. This is true up to a point, but other factors, including the deaths of two of his children, contributed to a long pause in his writing. He always observed the sacraments and was in due course reconciled to the church hierarchy through Cardinal Vaughan, the archbishop of Westminster. As Hugh Tulloch has demonstrated for this period, Acton left the corrections in the church to the hands of God and turned his attention to a far worse and more immediate problem – that of nationalism.[32]

As his most complete biographer, Roland Hill, has pointed out, "Virtually alone among the liberals of his age, Acton saw where obsessions with class, race, and nationality would lead."[33] To combat the latter, he felt it was better that, rather than a single nation-state, several nations co-exist under the same state. In this, he preferred the old and slightly chaotic Austro-Hungarian Empire to the united Germany founded by Bismarck in 1870–1.

Now, if I may return directly to his work as a historian. With the founding in 1886 of the *English Historical Review*, England's first truly professional historical journal, along the German model, and with the appointment of a new Regius Professor of Modern History at Cambridge nine years later, the central figure in both cases being Acton, the profession took a quantum leap forward. However, as Hugh Tulloch has argued, Acton was critical, not subservient, to many aspects of modern German historiography.[34] For one, Acton detected too much predeterminism in what he saw as the huge influence of Hegel over his German colleagues. Not only was there an absence of contingency, choice, and chance in their histories, but also a metaphysical path leading to the worship of nationalist mythology and submission to temporal order in their thoughts. Acton sought his own brand of historical science based on ethics – an ethics based, in turn, on an Old and New Testament yardstick, which he believed was timeless and universalist. Was this idea to be an integral part of his unfinished *History of Liberty*? We shall never know.

Much has been made by Acton's detractors about this greatest book never written and his so-called overall failure in life, which is noted even in the *Dictionary of National Biography*. It is true that the great book was not produced, nor did he write any other books. However, with over 200 scholarly historical essays and numerous other published articles and reviews (as readily seen in J. Rufus Fears's massive three-volume compilation), he made a huge contribution both quantitatively and qualitatively to the study of modern history.[35]

As Hugh Tulloch has pointed out, Acton's actual applications of moral judgment were few and far between.[36] Acton also sought a science of character, a historical psychology, as it were – another reason for his admiring the writings of George Eliot – something never possible for Ranke in the researching of state papers in archives. To condemn a Borgia pope was a straightforward task, other judgments required much more digging to justify. Towards the end of his career, he became, if anything, more scrupulous in his writing. His inaugural lecture as Regius Professor contained 105 footnotes, referring to over 300 sources. His subsequent lectures on such topics as the French Revolution would trace all secondary references back to original published sources and governmental records. At times he even retried his previous cases in retrospect, finding, for example, the verdict in Mary Queen of Scots' involvement in her husband's murder as lacking sufficient evidence. The hanging judge could become the appeals judge. As Tulloch has concluded, Acton, in his own works, came to see that history was neither a purely inductive science nor wholly objective. In this, he may have anticipated the later criticisms of Ranke's methodology in general for its naiveté.

His final great endeavour as part of his vigorous rejuvenation of the School of History at Cambridge was, of course, the planning of the *Cambridge Modern History*, a multi-volume study of "universal history" – really European history – with himself as editor. In his instruction letter to over one hundred contributors, he urged the utmost effort in diligent research and impartiality. "Our scheme requires that nothing shall reveal the country, the religion, or the party to which the writers belong," he wrote, and "we shall avoid the needless utterance of opinion, and the service of a cause." "Our Waterloo must be one that satisfies French and English, Germans and Dutch alike." And in a possible strike at nationalism, he wrote concerning "universal" history, "It moves in a succession to which the nations are subsidiary. Their story will be told, not for their own sakes, but in reference and subordination to a higher series, according to the time and the degree in which they contribute to the common fortune of mankind."[37] Apart from his efforts to solicit contributors, his own contribution to the series remained unfinished. Stricken by illness he was forced to resign his professorship after only six years of service.

In Britain, there were always those who disliked him. The sheer diversity of his background led to nicknames such as the Professor (before he was one), the German, and the Neapolitan. His Catholicism brought him difficulties, from his rejection for admission to Cambridge University as a teenager, to the puzzlement of his colleagues in being both a liberal and a Catholic, to his willingness to take part in the public processions of the small Catholic community of Cambridge in the full academic regalia of Regius Professor of Modern History. He was never apologetic about his background or beliefs. And he could be critical of his country as he could of any country that engaged in evil things. As he stated, "In judging our national merits we must allow much for national hypocrisy. Where ever we went, we were the best colonizers in the world – but we exterminated the natives where ever we went, and what of our governing of Ireland, of India – opium in China."[38]

To historians, he continued to urge the path of the "inflexible integrity of the moral code."[39] Beware of too much explaining, lest we end by too much excusing, he often quoted from Madame de Staël. And, as he also stated, never forget "the degrading misery of the poor; the horror of the battlefield; the scenes of the hospital; the smallness, selfishness and cowardice of great men; the depravity of wealth."[40] The duty of the historian includes speaking for those who have no voice, the dispossessed, those defeated in a good cause.

Spending most of his last days at his Bavarian estate, largely because of its more benign climate, he died there in 1902. Though plans were launched for his body to be placed in the impressive family vault at Aldenham, Acton was buried at his request in a small cemetery near his Bavarian home, where a daughter had been buried after her tragic death years earlier.

The inevitable public memorial services followed back in England, as well as tributes in Germany, where he had been awarded an honorary degree by Munich. Though tributes may have been many, the ultimate statement of the worthiness of a public figure for eternal praise was, as perhaps it is still, an obituary in the *Times* of London.[41] While listing Acton's many accomplishments, the paper could not resist in making the criticism of his lack of national fibre. For Acton, in his resistance to the dangers of nationalism and imperialism, perhaps he would have regarded this as praise.

The Question of Moral Judgment after Acton

As we have seen, Acton in his own times had differences with both Ranke and Dollinger over the exercise of moral judgment in history. These differences extended to many others, including Mandell Creighton – who otherwise had been so important to Acton as a co-founder of the *English Historical Review*.

Various historians in many camps disputed Acton's ideas. Although he was respected as a religious man, many Christian historians had a strong aversion to his position – none more than Dom David Knowles (1896–1974), a Benedictine who eventually became Regius Professor of Modern History at Cambridge (1954–63). A distinguished medieval historian, Knowles also served for a period as the chair of the Faculty of History at Cambridge. He was particularly gifted in his writing for his analysis of the character of some of the great figures of the Middle Ages such as Archbishop Thomas Becket. Yet Knowles, while still a student at Cambridge, may well have been the first to hurl the epithet of "hanging judge" at Acton. As Knowles later wrote with respect to human history, "The degree of ignorance, the degree of malice, the degree of weakness, the degree of guilt, must always elude us. The whole concept of the historian as a judge in a trial is radically false, if only because a judge by his very office deals only with accused or impleaded persons; he condemns or acquits, he does not praise or reward. The historian's task is very different, he contemplates the whole of his world; he does not apportion guilt ... he presents what he sees."[42]

Herbert Butterfield, a lay Methodist and contemporary of Knowles, was also at one point Regius Professor of Modern History at Cambridge. He wrote and said much more directly about moral judgment in history, but in a less clear, more convoluted way. While a life-long admirer of Acton, he made it clear in *The Whig Interpretation of History* (1931) that he disagreed with his position on the matter of the historian's duty to make moral judgments. For Butterfield, the professional historian had to avoid moral judgments, as the most heightened of judgments.[43] It was not the task of the historian to make pronouncements of good or evil upon the actions of peoples in the past. According to C.T. McIntire, Butterfield believed such pronouncements to be wrong, both in terms of the competence area of historical study and as it was usurping the role of God – judge not, that you may not be judged.[44]

Later Butterfield, in his essay entitled "Moral Judgments in History" in *History and Human Relations* (1951), gave his most complete account of his objections to such judgments. An earlier work, *Christianity and History* (1949), had not dwelt much on moral judgments but had made it clear that one must not recklessly render judgments on nations such as modern Germany. Butterfield believed that the principal task of academic historians was the production of "technical history." This entailed constructions based on concrete facts in the fashion of science. Technical history was concerned only with externals, not the inner workings of human affairs. His 1951 essay was in part an attempt to clarify what, for some of his critics, was his seeming advocacy of history as an amoral discipline.

Butterfield made it clear that he reaffirmed his belief that one must not make moral judgments against individuals in history – "the historian can never quite know men from the inside."[45] His stance against judging events or institutions was more ambiguous, at times reverting to the position taken in his previous writings that judgments against states can be political judgments in the guise of moral judgments. At the same time, as McIntire has pointed out, he tried to provide some sort of qualifier for technical history having no ethical character and, in so doing, he gave "himself permission, in his role as historian, to denounce certain human actions as morally wrong."[46] Yet, Butterfield cautioned the historian not to frame descriptions into narratives with the specific purpose of arguing a matter of right and wrong. For McIntire, the contradictions only increased in Butterfield's subsequent attempts at clarifying his position.

Butterfield did not write about these questions in the easiest of times, given his involvement in contemporary European diplomacy as well as diplomatic history, especially after a more complete revelation of the horrors of Nazi Germany following its defeat in 1945. Isaiah Berlin seemed to be the philosopher-historian more in keeping with the age, seeing the duty of the historian to morally judge the Hitlers and Napoleons for their massacres – such a mandate seemingly originating from a suffering humanity itself.

Recently, historians such as Adrian Oldfield and Jonathan Gorman have reopened the issue of the moral duties of historians. Oldfield makes the important distinction between moral outrage and moral judgment – the latter being a considered opinion, arrived at after carefully weighing evidence. He then notes and responds to the objections made by a number of prominent historians against making moral judgments. In relation to Herbert Butterfield, Oldfield doubts that any human being, past or present, could avoid making moral judgments. Furthermore, like all historical judgments, they are provisional – subject to further evidence. And finally, he objects to the notion that some actions of past figures are "natural" – suggesting some sort of determinism. More generally, Oldfield objects to the idea that it would be better for non-historians to pass judgments of a moral nature when historians are hard pressed to do so. And he wonders how the historian who is intent on following the advice of E.H. Carr can avoid making judgments on individuals such as Hitler and concentrate only on wider movements. Oldfield concludes that the historian "cannot avoid acting, from time to time, as moral educator."[47]

Jonathan Gorman argues along the same line but expands even more on the ethical responsibilities of the historian seeking and telling objective truth. Included in the re-creation of the past is the application of "moral understanding," which is "by no means the preserve of moral philosophers." This is part of the obligation to reveal truth both for the sake of the living and the dead (a point made by Acton). If historians feel inadequate for this task, Gorman suggests, perhaps they should receive more professional training in ethics.[48]

Perhaps E.H. Carr, in the old standby *What Is History?*, provides a pragmatic and realistic way out by noting that historical facts "presuppose some measure of interpretation; and historical interpretations always involve moral judgements."[49] However, Carr's formula de-emphasized the important element of individual will. Concerning the role of the individual in history, as Gertrude Himmelfarb points out, if one denies the possibility of heroism in history, one also denies the possibility of villainy.[50] In such instances, a determinism sets in, which presents as inaccurate a sense of an ordinary person as it does of kings and prime ministers.

In another important area, that of emotion, compromise approaches as advocated by historians such as Carr are as unsatisfactory as they were in the case of truth. Mark Salber Phillips, in his recent book *On Historical Distance*, points out instances of sentimental history, of compassionate narratives, in early modern and modern history. In referring to the work of historians such as Robert Soloman, he makes the important point that reason and emotion need not be confrontational.[51] History is, after all, about ourselves, including those who were dispossessed in various ways. This notion includes a redemptive quality often found in such works as E.P. Thompson, *The Making of the English Working Class* (1963). But advocacy of particular causes through historical writing, where people in past lives can be grouped as victims on the side of the angels or as oppressive devils (i.e., opponents of the cause), should not be confused with moral judgments in the fullest sense. And the special obligation to speak out for the oppressed, long forgotten in the pages of conventional historical narratives, was a powerful message in the writings of Acton.

Moral Progress

It can be taken for granted that, for those who emphasized the accident in history or who accepted in large measure the cyclical view of history, there was no pattern of moral progress throughout the ages. On the other hand, for Christians and liberal-rationalists, the passage of time meant moving towards some predetermined goal – in the case of the former, union with the Creator; for the latter, the triumph of reason in a fully free society. Acton's hopes, of course, were a mixture of both. With conservative Christians and their emphasis on original sin, the path would also end in glory but with considerably more detours.

Goldwin Smith, who wrote a good deal about moral progress in modern history, equated it with advancing character in individuals.[52] In his early writings as a liberal Anglican, he argued that Christianity had greatly added to the moral progress of the modern world, with such progress being "the cardinal element of the three elements of human progress – the other two being the intellectual and the productive (or virtue, knowledge, and industry)."[53] Prior to 1880, Smith had systematically argued against not only conservative High Churchmen such as J.L. Mansel but also the followers of Comte, the original positivists, in their predictions about the collapse of Christianity. Later moving towards a position of agnosticism, he maintained more of a culturalist view of Christianity, still recognizing its social utility but with less confidence in its future.[54] Acton, in contrast, maintained his belief in Christianity and its ultimate triumphal union with rationality at the end.

In the twentieth century, Christian apologists for moral progress became less evident, still perhaps hoping that the ultimate spiritual goal of their religion would be achieved but acknowledging the enormous global setbacks for morality in that century. Increasingly, it seems that the mantle of optimism has passed to scientists and the New Atheists.

Michael Shermer, in his book *The Moral Arc: How Science Makes Us Better People* (2015), traces how scientific reasoning, developed from the Age of Reason and the Enlightenment, is progressively being applied to non-scientific disciplines and areas of social concern. He boldly lists twelve categories in which the world has become a better place as a result of this process. As we have already seen, scientists such as Richard Dawkins and Sam Harris as New Atheists are ready to supply an even clearer direction in their moral systems, sharing many values with the old religions. In so doing, they become public moralists willing to project an ongoing continuum of moral progress from the past through the present to the future. Thus the virtue of hope is joined to an emotional demand for justice. Bertrand Russell, one of Britain's greatest philosophers, and an agnostic, viewed moral statements as expressions of attitudes and desires rather than objective truths.[55]

A.C. Grayling has made the point that ongoing work in neuroscience may conclude that free will is "an Illusion." Certainly so much of the justification for making moral judgments with respect to people, past and present, has depended on the concept of free will – at least for Christians and people of Abrahamic faiths in general. Yet Grayling defends the concept of free will as a good idea, even on non-religious grounds.[56] At least for the time being, there seems to be some consensus for its retention.

Suggested Readings

Herbert Butterfield, "Moral Judgments in History," in Butterfield, *History and Human Relations*, 101–30 (London: Collins, 1951)

Richard Dawkins, *The God Delusion* (New York: Houghton Mifflin, 2008)

William Dray, "Philosophy and Historiography," *Companion to Historiography*, edited by Michael Bentley, 763–82 (London: Routledge, 1997)

Jonathan Gorman, *Historical Judgement: The Limits of Historiographical Choice* (Montreal and Kingston: McGill-Queen's University Press, 2008)

A.C. Grayling, *The God Argument: The Case against Religion and for Humanism* (New York: Bloomsbury, 2013)

Dom David Knowles, *The Historian and Character* (Cambridge: Cambridge University Press, 1963)

Paul T. Phillips, *The Controversialist: An Intellectual Life of Goldwin Smith* (Westport, CT: Praeger, 2002)

Hugh Tulloch, *Acton* (New York: St. Martin's Press, 1988)

chapter three

Meaning

As with truth and morality, any consideration of an overall meaning to history entails some emotional element. Not so much nostalgia, it potentially is linked to the search for a meaning to life itself. It also entails concepts, measurements, and perceptions of time, the possible influence of laws of the physical universe, the inheritance of cultural or biological traits resulting in predictable patterns of behaviour, and the idea of higher, possibly spiritual, powers, providing direct or indirect guidance to actions of individuals and communities through time.

If causation, especially single causation, is pursued too vigorously, as the key to understanding the movement of history, the historian can be accused of imposing a determinism on human actions. However, Marc Bloch makes the prudent point that "historical facts" are "in essence, psychological facts" and normally "find their antecedents in other psychological facts." Bloch notes that "history seeks for causal wave-trains and is not afraid, since life shows them to be so, to find them multiple."[1] Under these conditions, especially moving beyond single-cause explanations, there is less chance of compromising the idea of free will. Would that was always the case!

At the opposite end of the spectrum from emphasis on causation, and the accompanying danger of being charged with determinism, is the belief that history, beyond the recitation of bare facts, becomes a form of delusion in the construction of elaborate causal narratives. Such a position has been adopted by those who see history, like life, as merely a succession of accidents without any further meaning. Closely related to this is contingency, which sees many possible paths through time that could have been taken as easily as others. Contingency, and especially accident, is most difficult to accept for any historians who would move beyond pure antiquarianism. Yet, according to R.W. Davies, an inspection of E.H. Carr's notes towards a second edition of *What Is History?* reveals a much greater emphasis on accident.[2] But the perception of an overwhelming element of chance in our lives is nevertheless the experience of many of us, much to the intellectual consternation of many historians, as well as believers in most religions. I also believe that it, much like the thought of a chaotic universe, can produce fear in many of us.

Background

Since ancient times, those who would claim to be historians have attempted to apply overall designs to human actions through time. Broadly speaking, their patterning can be divided into two general views: the recurring or cyclical and the linear towards some predetermined ending. There were other shorter measurements, such as yearly repetitious or extended calendars helpful to agriculture or religious observances or astronomy and astrology. Occasionally some civilizations might not measure time to any degree; in one rare case, a tribe – the Amondawa of South America – had no concept or word for "time." Mircea Eliade in *The Myth of the Eternal Return* (1954) describes the theory of great cosmic cycles involving belief in the regular destruction of the universe followed in timely fashion by its re-creation. According to Eliade, this theme is traceable from the Atharva Veda to old Germanic traditions, confirming the Indo-Aryan structure of this widespread myth.[3] Humanity magically re-enters sacred time in the myth of eternal return. Even early Judaism originally operated in this world until a concept, imprecisely measured at that, of relatively short stages of "history" developed from creation to the end of time. Traces could also be seen in some secular chronicles of Roman history as part of the

Greco-Oriental world of ideas. Eventually a more modern concept of historical time broke through the prevailing yearning to remain in a mythical age, exposing people to a form of linear measurement that seemed empty of inherent value. It produced a "terror of time" in ancient peoples. However, in Christianity, the value of historical time was raised to an article of faith seen in its passage from creation through to Christ's second coming, supplying support against the terror of time through the resurrection of all believers.[4] As Eliade describes it, "Thus Christian thought tended to transcend, once and for all, the old themes of eternal repetition, just as it had undertaken to transcend all the other archaic viewpoints by revealing the importance of the religious experience of faith and that of the value of the human personality."[5]

Early Christian writers down to St. Augustine saw a straight line from the "fall of man" to the final redemption through the incarnation and death of Jesus. Consequently, cyclical time as a concept was abolished in favour of a linear concept of time and history. The central facts of history were never repeated. Christ dies but once!

This is not to say that schema for seeing patterns in history that might recur, in a subordinate way, cannot be detected from Vico to Arnold Toynbee. But the linear, progressive view has prevailed down to the present day in the Abrahamic religions, especially Christianity, and has also formed the majoritarian view of history in modern minds in its secularized counterpart of the linear, progressive concept arising from the Scientific Revolution and the Enlightenment to the present. Thus St. Augustine and Bossuet share the idea of a "happy ending" with Condorcet, Saint-Simon, and Buckle.

Providence

Providence, or Divine Providence, is the Judeo-Christian belief that God exercises an overall superintendence not only in the course of history but also in the lives of individuals. Adherents to this doctrine point to at least three statements in Proverbs: "In all your ways acknowledge him, and he will make straight your path" (3:6); "Commit your work to the Lord, and your plans will be established" (16:30); and "A man's mind plans his way, but the Lord directs his steps" (16:9). Such statements have not been taken as mere metaphors by Christians: they have been part of their unique views of history. And their underlying doctrine has posed problems such as how to reconcile such a narrative with the moral accountability following from the idea of free will. If God operates within history, does he press his knowledge of the future upon humankind, thus compromising his final judgment of our moral actions as well as the future course of history? Apart from a handful of Christian philosophers such as Arthur Peacocke, who claims God does not know the future, most believe that free will can be reconciled with God's foreknowledge through his omnipotence and omniscience. John Polkinghorne believes God knows the future but does not make it. According to this view, God is beyond the understanding of humans, not being human. Yet in the concept of the Trinity and Incarnation, does He not also share at least in part in human nature?

The same might be said of the classic problems of theodicy – how can we explain God's obvious permission for the operations of evil as well as disasters, while He acts as the loving governor of the universe? To explain these things in fully human terms has challenged believers since the writing of the book of Job. Could God be part evil and part good, or perhaps two gods or principles (one evil and one good) as held by Zoroastrians? For non-believers, it added to their dislike of Christianity, as in James Mill's comment to his son John Stuart Mill that the Christian concept of God was essentially that of a wicked entity.

For the Abrahamic religions, acceptance of this basic, though paradoxical, situation ultimately rested on faith in revealed religion. In the High Middle Ages, this was supplemented, in the case of Christianity, by Scholastic arguments, including those of St. Thomas Aquinas, using reason as a supporting mechanism. By the early modern period, faith began to wear thin, as described by Charles Taylor in *A Secular Age* (2007). As the world became "disenchanted," the idea of humankind moving towards the fulfilment of God's plan assisted by Divine interactions with human communities and individuals became less convincing for some. Through the Scientific Revolution and eventually the Enlightenment, a secular version of the linear, progressive view of history emerged, thanks to the Judeo-Christian model already ingrained in Western thinking.

For a very few historians hostile to Christianity, such as David Hume, a secular, progressive view can be traced early and eventually down to August Comte and historians such us Henry Thomas Buckle. However, for most historians and other thinkers, this secular view entailed a transitional phase, which Taylor has described as "Providential Deism,"[6] lasting roughly from the mid-seventeenth to the late eighteenth centuries. In this process, reason, rather than the direct prescriptive role of God, came to serve as a basis of morality, although reason was seen as God-given. Instead of God's active intervention, human reason did the heavy lifting, to the same end – the advance of morality among humans. An outstanding figure here was Immanuel Kant. Though personally a devout Christian, Kant shifted the advance of morality to the liberation of reason. The Categorical Imperative was the basis of the new order, designed to be intellectually as well as morally pleasing, unlike the less lofty benefits to ourselves and others in the observance of the Golden Rule. By 1800, Providential Deism ended in a further transition to exclusive humanism for many thinkers. Thus, ironically, humanists, including atheists and agnostics, in their pursuit of a new directing force in history had Christian roots. For most other people, however, including historians, Providence continued to function in their basic thinking in relation to their general view of history and as a guide in their personal lives (often through prayer). This trend extended even into the twentieth century for some historians and for many Christians.

Modified Providence

For some historians who were devout Christians and disciples of Ranke, the new scientific history could be combined with a modified concept of Providence in accordance with secular political developments. For Acton, Providence meant progress. Herbert Butterfield maintained his belief in Providence into the late twentieth century. As he stated in his well-known book *Christianity and History* (1949), "Whether we are Christians or not, whether we believe in a Divine Providence or not, we are liable to serious technical errors if we do not regard ourselves as born into a providential order."[7] In committing this "technical error," Butterfield believed historians would lose an "added dimension" in historical science, although he granted that the much greater loss was in their spiritual life.[8] At the same time, while maintaining his belief in the searching aspects of belief in Divine Providence, he freely admitted as an adherent to the scientific method in history in the fashion of Ranke that the pursuit of "technical" history would provide no meaning to life.[9] History was ultimately a personal experience. As a Christian, he stated, "I am unable to see how a man can find the hand of God in secular history, unless he has first found that he has an assurance of it in his personal experience" and "in this science our interpretation of the human drama throughout the ages rests finally on our interpretation of our most private experience of life, and stands as merely an extension of it."[10] Butterfield in subsequent writings acknowledged the complexities of maintaining such a position and urged the "absolutely necessary concomitant of historical study" in "intellectual humility" in regard to the various techniques and differing philosophies of other historians.[11]

Butterfield was always a strong advocate for the idea of the importance of the individual in history, pointing to the differences between belief in Providence and determinism. But increasingly his position was very much a minority one. Certainly, by the time he was writing, most historians, like most people, saw the hand of God in little. Butterfield ascribed this short-sightedness to "a misunderstanding of the scientific method," giving people "a too mechanical and too abstract idea of God – one which fails to do justice to his fullness and richness." For Butterfield, we "must not imagine that God created the universe in the way we analyze it – more likely he resembled the composer who, we might say, was just out to create a beautiful thing."[12] As the composer, God could see where it all is going, for ourselves we were playing but an instrument, and for the first time at that.[13]

Butterfield made the astute observation that "the twentieth century saw the human race gain possession of forms of power so colossal that previous generations, in their wildest dreams, had had no inkling of such possibilities. It saw the human race acquire forms of knowledge which made men almost feel themselves gods, feel that the human mind was the monarch of the universe … Men even imagined that they could play Providence for themselves, control the course of history, and mould the shape of the whole future."[14] Certainly this was an apt description of Julian Huxley's "evolutionary humanism," a sort of secular religion in which an informed elite of scientists collectively would become a god, thereby removing the possibility of humanity descending into chaos with the knowledge that there was no God in the traditional sense. Evolutionary humanism was one of those comforting concepts in dealing with the intelligentsia's fear of the untrustworthy masses following the announcement of God's death.[15] Unfortunately, God's death also opened, as Butterfield anticipated, problems stemming from the wickedness in human nature leading to the likes of dictatorships or dystopias, as described in novels or in films such as *Forbidden Planet* (1956) revealing the enhanced destructive possibilities of the id. But historians were not in the position of combating such outcomes on their own. Recently in literature and cinema there has been the trend to replace God with extraterrestrials providing guidance to the human race. A very good example of this is the film *2001* (1968). Here again the intention seems to be to combat fear.

In another direction, determinism began its upward climb in secular philosophies that replaced Divine Providence looking for a prevailing pattern in history. Of these, the most pre-eminent inspirer was Georg Wilhelm Friedrich Hegel (1770–1831). Here the concept of free will was at much more risk than was the case with Providence. For Hegel, like Kant, progress involved emergent rationality in human beings. There could be setbacks, of course, but these were explained in the dynamic principle of the dialectic. As reason and freedom would eventually prevail, history would become meaningful. Young Hegelians – or idealists, as they were also termed in Britain – would follow in Hegel's path. Their work led to expansions of his theory from the realm of pure ideas to social classes and to a more far-reaching analysis of history in another German philosopher, Karl Marx (1818–1883).

Marx's dialectical materialism provided a mechanism to explain the driving force and overall secular/progressive view (if not attempted prophesy) of human affairs for many years to come. Butterfield considered Marxism to be "the most formidable threat to Christianity today," "wisely based upon an interpretation of history." He "personally was disposed to trust that challenge as both a dangerous and respectable one."[16] Decades later, Gertrude Himmelfarb wondered if postmodernism would last after its novelty had worn off, but saw in its blend with Jürgen Habermas's Frankfurt school of thought a "linguistic version of Marxism" with far more possibility of its influence and endurance.[17]

Marxism as a school of historical thought has also served as a model for a host of advocacy views of history, from the modified version by E.P. Thompson, which seeks to bring the working class into the foreground of history as active agents, to women's history, ethnic history, gay history, and so on.

Philosophy of History and Historiography

Since the Enlightenment, there have been other ways of finding meaning in or paths to history besides Providence or the secular equivalents discussed so far. The "science of history" approach was modified into the "science of the spirit" by the Italian idealist philosopher Benedetto Croce (1866–1952). R.G. Collingwood (1889–1943) saw history as a recollection of past thinking, also challenging positivist approaches. In turn, positivism reappeared in the literary works of H.G. Wells (1866–1946) both in fiction and in his *Outline of History* (as a single volume, 1920). But these efforts, largely by philosophers, coincided with a new era in history writing that attempted to take in global developments under the rubric of world history. The roots of such histories go back a very long way to the earliest works, such as those of the Chinese and Greeks. But such works were really about the people who wrote them, as was the Old Testament, which purported to be a history of humankind but in reality was an exclusivist narrative of God's relationship with the Hebrews.

The effort to create a "world history," of course, was renewed with the European voyages of discovery from the sixteenth century as well as the interest in creating models of alternate ethical behaviour from that period into the Enlightenment. It was also encouraged by the goal of Ranke and his disciples to write so-called universal history, which was actually in its inception the history of Europe (in fact, often only the compilation of national histories, in the case of Ranke). With the new empirical framework of research in archives or using primary printed sources, as well as the practical framework of manageable size and some sort of conscious or unconscious perspective, this limited production was, at least for much of the remainder of the nineteenth century, all that was possible. Efforts to include the Americas, Asia, and Africa gradually increased, leading to such publications as *The Book of History: A History of All Nations from the Earliest Time to the Present* (1915–21), by James Bryce, Holland Thompson, and W.M. Flinders Petrie.

As with early efforts in the field of comparative religion, such works could often reveal ultimately offensive biases against the non-European world, as with the racist notions that Flinders Petrie applied in his studies of Egypt. Ultimately, these early efforts gave birth to the textbooks in Western civilization and later global or world history so familiar to generations of twentieth-century college students. Kenneth Clark's *Civilization* series, which debuted on television at the end of the 1960s, followed the same path, with an enormous number of imitators, and ultimately fathered the History Channel.

Suspicions about and hostility towards philosophies of history began with Ranke and his historicism and that of many of his disciples. They increased with the expansion of the empiricism of the newly founded discipline with its emphasis on subject specialists. Yet this specialization also coincided with the popular interest in a global perspective by the end of the nineteenth century. How could such a perspective be maintained, given the mandate to search archives and primary printed sources in scrupulous detail? The consensus was that, in any possible historical undertaking, hypotheses ought not to be drawn ready-made from the work of philosophers. By the twentieth century, this consensus had given birth to the field of historiography, in which historians would discuss broader historical approaches, as opposed to the philosophy of history, which became a subfield of philosophy.

No historian wanted to replicate the mistake of Ranke's contemporary Heinrich Leo (1799–1878), a fellow Prussian historian, a Lutheran, and ultimately a conservative, who for an extended period fell under the sway of Hegel. If philosopher's ideas were to be applied to history, they must be carefully verified empirically. And it was preferable if the philosophers in question also wrote history, not works using history as a mere illustration of their philosophical thinking. The underlying themes that did emerge in the quest for global history were rather simple, such as the advance of human achievements through rationalist thinking, as seen in popular college survey textbooks such as Edward McNall Burns's *Western Civilizations* (numerous editions since 1941) or in *The Story of Civilizations* by Will and Ariel Durant (11 volumes, 1935–75).

The most ambitious undertakings of this type of work, with the most intellectually challenging writing, were those of a group in the early to mid-twentieth century known as the metahistorians – principally Christopher Dawson (1889–1970), Arnold J. Toynbee (1889–1975), and, to a lesser degree, Oswald Spengler (1880–1936). Notwithstanding the Spengler's less clear title as a historian, he was the earliest inspirer of the genre. His book *The Decline of the West*, circulating eventually in two volumes in the 1920s, predicted the collapse of Western civilization. Using examples from a number of world civilizations, Spengler predicted that such a collapse would come to pass after "an age of Caesarism." More of a philosopher and social commentator than historian, he took the reading public in Germany, Britain, and other countries by storm, although he did not impress all historians with his non-scientific, non-empirical methodology. However, he did briefly become a celebrity intellectual and inspired many.

His world view of history certainly influenced two young British historians, Christopher Dawson and Arnold Toynbee.

Christopher Dawson began his career with solid credentials, specifically in the field of history (honours BA in modern history, Oxford 1911). Although he subsequently studied economics and theology, he saw himself primarily as a cultural historian. Interested in the history of civilization, he published his first book, *The Age of the Gods*, in 1928. It was intended to be one of five books chronicling European history to the twentieth century. Unfortunately, ill health and distractions in other areas of history and other activities such as participation in the Sword of the Spirit movement prevented him from obtaining his ultimate goal. Nonetheless, he was a prolific writer, although he only sporadically held academic appointments. He was elected a Fellow of the British Academy in 1943.

A Catholic convert, Dawson firmly believed that the roots of Modern Europe could be found in medieval Catholicism – and this thesis formed the basis of many of his writings. Unlike Spengler, he had hopes for the survival and revival (as well as unity) of the West, especially in the dark days of the Second World War, through its reconnecting with its Christian Catholic roots. He also believed "historic Christianity" to be "far more than any purely rational creed where the 'Religion of Progress' finds its satisfaction."[18] It was also best for the world as a whole. In what was possible a reference to a book by Julian Huxley, Dawson argued that,

> A religion without Revelation is a religion without History, and it is just the historical element in Christianity which gives it its peculiar character, and differentiates it from the unprogressive metaphysical religions of the East. A purely rational religion must inevitably become a metaphysical religion, for the religious impulse can find no nourishment for itself in the arid and narrow region of the discursive reason, and it is only in the metaphysical sphere – in the intuition of an absolute and eternal truth – that religion and reason can meet.[19]

Dawson influenced a host of writers, including T.S. Eliot but especially Roman Catholics such as the economist Barbara Ward and historian Martin C. D'Arcy. He also had many involvements with Catholic writers in other disciplines, such as the philosopher Jacques Maritain in the 1920s and 1930s. But in such involvements Dawson made clear that his approach to issues was always that of the historian.[20] Dawson also acted as a sort of John the Baptist to the messiah role of Toynbee in the cause of metahistory, in both coining and defining the term.

Arnold J. Toynbee: The Historian as Prophet

The most complete example of metahistorian – and, indeed, of any full-fledged historian in the past century who attempted to provide an overall meaning to the history of civilizations – is Arnold J. Toynbee. Since its completion in the 1960s, his work, in length at least, has not been matched by any historian. Toynbee deserves the special consideration that now follows.

There are few examples of an academic scholar who rose so high in the esteem of the general public only to experience such a precipitous fall as Toynbee. Some of the explanation for his fall can certainly be placed at the feet of jealousy and personal dislike on the part of his fellow historians. But most, I think, can be explained by the grandiose role he fashioned for himself, with the inherent risks in such an undertaking. The result was more than merely a sad ending to an incredible career; it also had a stifling effect on future initiatives in an area within the discipline of history that is worthy of further exploration.

Ambition is certainly a constant theme in Toynbee's life, and he exhibited it quite early. Born into a striving middle-class family and named after an uncle who was a prominent economist and Christian socialist at Oxford, Toynbee entered Winchester School with great hopes of academic success. He easily lived up to the expectations of his parents, later being admitted to that major pathway for future academics, politicians, and public servants, Balliol College, Oxford. In 1911, he graduated with a distinguished first in classics, already catching the eye of leading academics with his unusually high proficiency in languages both ancient and modern. Within two years, he was a fellow and tutor in ancient history at Balliol as well as being engaged to the daughter of one of England's most prominent intellectuals, Gilbert Murray, Regius Professor of Greek at Oxford. Toynbee received numerous prizes and honours, allowing him to travel to Greece for additional archaeological training in Athens as well as supporting an impressive early list of publications in his field.

With the outbreak of the First World War, Toynbee found his travel plans curtailed as well as his scholarly work redirected. It could have been much more so if he had undertaken military service, of course. According to his principal biographer, William H. McNeill, he avoided this duty in a duplicitous manner by offering himself for military service publicly while privately prodding his physician to offer rather lame excuses for his rejection by the armed services. While these manoeuvrings worked, he suffered considerable guilt in the long run, which perhaps drove him into other forms of service and into a lifetime of trying to justify to the public the benefits of his hard work.[21]

In 1917, Toynbee was appointed to the Intelligence Department of the Foreign Office. This followed his publications in 1915 and 1916 on aspects of the war, including the treatment of Armenians in the Ottoman Empire. He also resigned his fellowship at Balliol. In 1918–19, he was in the British delegation to the Paris Peace Conference. Though immersed in current affairs, he was offered and accepted a newly created chair in modern Greek and Byzantine history at London, funded by the Greek government and a group of subscribers in Britain. Soon after, he journeyed with his wife to Greece and Turkey to observe the early stages of the war that had erupted between the two countries. The result was a turning point in Toynbee's career.

While touring battle sites and fully expecting to see fresh examples of Turkish barbarism, the Toynbees in fact encountered evidence of Greek army atrocities committed against the Turks. The subsequent reports penned by Toynbee eventually forced his resignation from the Koraes Chair of Greek history in 1924. Influential friends immediately helped at this point. Already with a temporary position at the Institute of International Affairs at Chatham

House in London, eventually he was able to combine that work with a chair in international history at the University of London. Through astute negotiations, his position at the institute was elevated to director of studies and he was able to retain his professorship in international history, which itself was transformed to a research professorship by 1928. The agreement hammered out by 1928 involved no teaching (which he never liked) and salary from both the university and the institute (something resented by his University of London colleagues until his retirement in the mid-1950s). His sole duty, as it had been since 1924, was the production of one volume per year for the Survey of International Affairs at Chatham House. It was a task perfectly suited to his expanding world interests and soon blended into the information gathering for what would be the greatest project of his life, a mega-volume comparative study of history. As Toynbee put it, "I could not, I believe, have done either piece of work if I had not been doing the other at the same time. A survey of current affairs on a world-wide scale can be made only against a background of world-history; and a study of world-history would have no life in it if it left out the history of the writer's own lifetime."[22]

With a staff of secretaries to clip newspaper columns and provide other assistance, his role at Chatham House was largely supervisory, except for the writing of summaries. In this supervisory role, he would, after 1929, be assisted by Veronica Boulter, who ultimately took on a larger share of the writing of the annual survey. She was at Chatham House to the end of his career, eventually becoming his second wife in 1946. Toynbee's position gave him ample time officially on summer vacations and unofficially, one suspects, throughout the year for what he called the Nonsense Book.

The "Nonsense Book" was Toynbee's code name to family and friends for what would be his twelve-volume *Study of History*. Although formal work began on the *Study* in 1927, its actual inception was thirteen years earlier. Toynbee explained that the onset of the Great War struck him, while teaching *Literae Humaniores* to undergraduates, as remarkably similar in impact to what Thucydides experienced during Peloponnesian War. He claimed later that this revelation was the origin of his contemporaneous comparative approach to the study of civilization as opposed to a chronological overview of history. The decision to use civilizations as the basic units of study was reinforced in planning notes from about 1921, dealing with the clash of Greek ideas with those of the empires of the Middle East made during his tour of battle lines between Greece and Turkey. In any case, Toynbee states, "the gist" of the study was in his mind by 1920, "because my first deliberate attempt at writing it was in that summer."[23]

That fall, Toynbee read Oswald Spengler's *The Decline of the West*, which confirmed for him that using civilizations (eight in Spengler's work as opposed to twenty-one in Toynbee's) as the basic units of study in a comparative approach was correct, although it briefly unnerved him that Spengler might have rendered his whole inquiry redundant. However, upon further examination, Toynbee could not accept Spengler's "German a priori method," together with his dogmatic determinism and lack of "English empiricism." H. Stuart Hughes, Spengler's biographer, also believes readers were presented in the *Study* with a work of good temper, compared with the doomsday quality of *Decline of the West*.[24]

The first three volumes of Toynbee's *A Study of History* were completed by 1933. In these volumes, he advanced his mechanism for the origins of civilizations in what he called "challenge and response" (sometimes described as adversity theory). He claimed such an approach was a product of his interest in mythology – Mephistopheles's challenge to God and God's response in Goethe's *Faust*. In the inception of civilizations, Toynbee argued, adverse physical or social conditions had to be present to bring into being a creative minority who would, in its response to these challenges, provide direction and organization to the rest of the culture. But the challenge had to be the right balance, or golden mean, of stimuli – neither too insignificant nor too excessive. In turn, this pattern would spark the growth of more elaborate and significant organization and progress through the centuries, as long as the creative minority at the top remained creative. Toynbee placed the ultimate success of the civilization in the hands of this minority, not in the overall control of the environment or in their response to sudden external challenges (as he explored in volume 3). If creativity ceased, the creative minority would become simply the dominant minority, increasingly demanding loyalty and inflicting repression on the proletarian majority within and outside its frontiers in so-called universal states. In Toynbee's framework, empires were treated as products of times of trouble, and universal states as manifestations of a pause prior to the impending death of a civilization. Volumes 4, 5, and 6 fully explored these stages, which Toynbee called the four beats of genesis, growth, breakdown, and disintegration. Although this cyclical pattern repeated itself through history, it was by no means inevitable: Toynbee from first to last was a proponent of free will.

Reviews in Britain of the earliest volumes were quite positive. Toynbee had sent drafts to J.L. Hammond, George Gooch, and to his father-in-law, Gilbert Murray, who had given their approval. The *Times Literary Supplement*, the *New Statesman*, and the Manchester *Guardian* praised them. Toynbee was offered an honorary degree from Oxford. The reviews of the next three volumes were also positive, pointing to their huge span of historical learning, but reviewers raised more doubts about his lines of argument and placing of facts into pre-determined schemes. But soon reactions were eclipsed by the onset of the Second World War.

In 1940, Toynbee personally experienced a change of heart and a new direction in his study. Closely related to his separation from his wife, Rosalind, was his path away from Roman Catholicism, which he had almost embraced prior to the war. He now reverted to the thought patterns of his childhood, placing Christianity at the apex of all other faiths, but not in a denominational sense. He never returned to his early Anglicanism but rather blended a generic Christianity with respect for the major non-Western religions, especially Buddhism.[25]

In his first six volumes, Toynbee considered the emergence of universal churches – the spiritual bonding of what he called the oppressed "internal proletariat" of universal states – as a means of spreading cultural influences from dying civilizations to budding ones (chrysalis of higher religions). The subsequent volumes did trace specific secular links between civilizations, which was pleasing to technical historians. However, McNeill describes the revised outline of 1946 as a "rather clumsy hybrid."[26] But Toynbee had come to consider his older view of the churches as merely transmitters of bits of one civilization to another as patronizing and incomplete. Civilizations, he came to believe, existed to serve churches, not vice versa, and, through the higher religions, the goal of human life, communion with God, was moving towards fulfilment.[27] What had been a generally cyclical view of civilizations, with small progress in links between declining and rising ones, became his own version of a linear, progressive view of all history.

But much work lay ahead, including the use of old notes dating back to the late 1920s. This phase of Toynbee's work, volumes 7–10 would not appear until 1954, with volume 11 (an atlas) and volume 12, *Reconsiderations*, not published until 1959 and 1961, respectively. In the immediate postwar period of the late 1940s, it was the reissuing of the first six volumes, especially to North American audiences, and especially an abridgement by D.C. Somervell, that would give Toynbee an extraordinary public following. This growing influence also forced a greater number of historians to offer more thorough assessments of the *Study*, which many had previously ignored, being buried in their topic and area specialties and, of course, the general distraction of the Second World War.

The skilful 600-page abridgement by D.C. Somervell could not have been better timed. Issued in late 1946 in Britain and early 1947 in the United States by Oxford University Press, it resulted in massive sales. By September 1947, over 100,000 copies had been sold in the United States alone. In this reception of Toynbee, H. Stuart Hughes saw the public seeking and being given a sense of perspective on the bewildering postwar world.[28] McNeill believes much the same, although he also points to the enthusiasm for Toynbee's first six volumes that gripped Henry Luce and key figures at his magazine, *Time*, as early as 1942. Toynbee's reputation was reinforced by Somervell's abridgement, which was praised by such influential publications as the *Atlantic Monthly*, *Life*, *Newsweek*, and the *New York Review of Books*. Given this coverage, it is not a great surprise that Toynbee made the cover of *Time* later in 1947.

However, it was somewhat problematic for reviews to find an apt description of what Toynbee was attempting to do, especially in the remaining volumes of the *Study*. This was soon supplied by his friend and contemporary Christopher Dawson in a series of exchanges with Allan Bullock in the earliest issues of *History Today*. Here, Dawson introduced "a new word and one which is as yet unfamiliar to the ordinary reader." The word was "metahistory," which he applied to his own works such as *The Age of the Gods* (1920) and *Progress and Religion* (1929) and that of Toynbee. As Dawson defined it:

> I take it that the term was coined on the analogy of Metaphysics which is itself by no means an easy word to define. When Aristotle had written his books on Physics, he proceeded to discuss the ultimate concepts that underlie his physical theories: the nature of matter, the nature of being and the cause of motion and change. In the same way Metahistory is concerned with the nature of history, the meaning of history and the cause and significance of historical change. The historian himself is primarily engaged in the study of the past. He does not ask himself why the past is different from the present or what is the meaning of history as a whole. What he wants to know is what actually happened at a particular time and place and what effect it had on the immediate future.[29]

Ten years later, in *Reconsiderations*, the final volume of the *Study*, Toynbee acknowledged that at least the last six volumes of his project were indeed metahistory, citing Dawson's definition. As Toynbee stated, "I should say myself that the present book began as an analytico-classifactory comparative study of human affairs and turned into a metahistorical inquiry en route."[30]

Indeed, it was obvious that, what had been latent in the first six volumes had become an explicit new direction in the next four. And what had become a steady growing trickle of criticism, chiefly in Britain, now became a tsunami. For many, this metahistory was not history; and, for some, the metahistorian was seen as a would-be prophet, a term of derision. Allan Bullock's exchange with Christopher Dawson in *History Today* in 1951, where Bullock publicly pointed out that a search for overall meaning in history was not the historian's job, paled in comparison with the rancour to follow.

This type of negative response was most famously seen in Hugh Trevor-Roper's devastating review entitled "Arnold Toynbee's Millennium" in *Encounter* in June 1957[31] – a turning point in Toynbee's career. But, oddly enough, as we shall see, the word "prophet" may have in fact been used first by Toynbee himself, and by some of his admirers, before it was adopted by his opponents. For Trevor-Roper, Toynbee had emerged as the prophet of a philosophy of messianic defeatism, believing that Western civilization would soon follow the pattern of self-destruction found in the twenty earlier civilizations Toynbee had described. According to Trevor-Roper, Toynbee believed that, in the Renaissance and Reformation period, with the embrace of rationalism, Western civilization had taken the wrong fork in the road. Now, after four hundred years, it was unlikely that there would be a return to the paradise of medieval innocence. Toynbee seemed to be proposing – or prophesizing – that the solution lay in the formation of a religion, largely Catholic Christian in origin, as the decline of the West was speeding up. Referring sarcastically to the "Old Testament" of the first four volumes of the *Study* and to the "New Testament" of the last volumes, Trevor-Roper depicted Toynbee as the willing accomplice of any force that would hasten this process of decline. Trevor-Roper observed that, in his work, Toynbee seemed to be taking on the role of messiah or founder of this last Universal Church, in which the best in Christianity would blend with the best in other world religions and show the path to God, which was, for Toynbee, the meaning and end of all history.

Trevor-Roper's article, which was more ridicule than analysis, came to be the best-known critique of Toynbee. But far more credible were the reviews of Pieter Geyl, professor of modern history at Utrecht. As early as the appearance of the first six volumes and abridgement, Geyl was already an arch-critic of Toynbee's work, although, unlike, Trevor-Roper, he avoided the path of personal insult (even calling Toynbee an apostle of gentleness) and, in turn, Toynbee was willing to engage in dialogue with him. Geyl argued that, while Toynbee's professed that he was engaged in empirical investigation, his methods were not those of the historian, and Geyl cited numerous examples of the cherry-picking of facts, especially in the early modern period of European history. In his view, Toynbee showed a lack of understanding "for the reality of the national factor in history." Moreover, in seeing "Western civilization" of one of twenty-one civilizations, which were the smallest "intelligible field of historical study," Toynbee was putting forward an "impossible, an impracticable demand."[32]

Detecting that Toynbee's view of history was "preeminently a spiritual one," even in his first six volumes, and that this focus neglected the importance of material changes and science to the historical process, at this stage (that is, before the next four volumes), Geyl nonetheless felt that Toynbee's method was "not intended to be that of the religious prophet."[33] At that time, Geyl's overall conclusion was that "Toynbee's system may not be so offensive as Spengler's ... but it is essentially no less irrational and aprioristic. By presenting it under the guise of scientific method and empiricism he not only revolts the scholar in me; he rouses me to protest, because I believe that clear thinking is perhaps the most crying need of our distracted world."[34]

Geyl was even more damning in "Toynbee the Prophet," following the publication of the next four volumes. For Geyl, these volumes made the nature of Toynbee's scheme much clearer, and he judged Toynbee's writing to be completely unhistorical, and his empirical investigation merely a "pretense." As Geyl states, "In reality he is a prophet revealing one all-meaning idea" – that is, "his dream of the unity of mankind in the love of God" – while denouncing the neo-paganism of Western intellectuals since the Renaissance. In conclusion, Geyl states, "This prophet usurps the name of historian," and "his prophecy is a blasphemy against Western Civilization." As proof of the delusion of being a prophet, Geyl cites Toynbee himself, in volume 10, referring to seven occasions when he was personally "transported" or "wrapped in communion with historic events or personages."[35]

Tangye Lean, a BBC producer and admirer of Toynbee's, may have added to the mounting evidence of Toynbee's self-delusion by quoting Toynbee's *Britain between West and East* (1946), where he stated that "poets and philosophers outrange the historians; while the prophets and the saints overtop and outlast them all."[36]

Reacting to such opinions in *Reconsiderations*, his ultimate rejoinder, Toynbee observed that he was not a prophet in any sense of the word. Geyl's verdict on that final volume was that "Toynbee appears to be more accessible to reason than I had expected ... He was doing his best to be a historian, but first and foremost he is still a prophet."[37]

Opposition to Toynbee mounted from all sorts of groups in this period. In Britain, the Reith Lectures for 1952, which Toynbee delivered on the BBC and later published under the title *The World and the West*, were taken by defenders of Britain's imperial past as an attack on the entire period of colonization rather than a plea to respect other cultures by ending the Western pretense of superiority. In suggesting that communism could be considered a spiritual force, Toynbee was also depicted by some as a believer both in the decline of the West and the death of Christianity. The lectures were thoroughly attacked by the Catholic journalist Douglas Jerrold in a pamphlet entitled "The Lie about the West," although Jerrold's conclusions were not shared by all of his co-religionists at the time.

With the publication of the last six volumes of the *Study*, some Christians rejoiced that Toynbee clearly adhered to an overall linear view of human history in the tradition of the Christian philosophers and historians of old and firmly away from cyclical concepts. But doubts began to be raised with his reference to his own peculiar agnosticism, as well his advocacy of syncretism in the form of a merger of Islam, Buddhism, and Hinduism with Christianity, albeit with the last as senior partner, in the ultimate Universal Religion. Among Catholics, fellow metahistorian Christopher Dawson regretted that this immense study had been "too telescopic," urging more specialized research to satisfy the doubters of his integrity as a historian.[38] American Dominican Linus Walker saw Toynbee as "a devoted historian of genius" who had been transformed into "prophet and preacher."[39]

For many Jews, Toynbee's frequent verbal attacks on the modern state of Israel by the early 1950s seemed to build on his view of Judaism as a "fossil survivor of extinct Syriac civilization" in the *Study*. The learned Abba Eban, then Israeli ambassador to the United States, stated, "Rising up in revolt against orthodox history, Professor Toynbee in a grandiose framework of the rise and fall of civilizations, presents the story of Israel over thousands of years as a grotesque psyche aberration leading to a squalid tragedy of injustice."[40] In spite of Toynbee's professions of friendship with Jewish intellectuals such as the historian Sir Lewis Namier, most observers would probably have agreed with the respected Christian theologian and historian Reinhold Niebuhr that Toynbee displayed a "deep-set prejudice against the Jews."[41]

Liberal rationalists, following the line of Trevor-Roper and Geyl, believed Toynbee had engaged in a perversion of history, noting his open hostility towards their number in his later volumes. Moreover, in reviewing his approach in making civilizations contemporary, many noted the parallel he drew between the so-called man worship of later Greek philosophy and that of humanists since the Renaissance (the notion of turning inward – extolling humans over the Divine).

In North America, once a bastion of support, Toynbee's popularity steadily declined. His seeming anti-Americanism on public issues by the 1960s did not help. And there were stories of his persistent bad behaviour, from his exploitive professional and family relationships in Britain to his thirst for lecture fees and visiting professorships in North America, with host colleges often left with a set of unhonoured obligations after the payment of large amounts of money.

Although he was undoubtedly a gifted writer (*Study* was translated into thirty languages), Toynbee's willingness to accept the description of being a poet (if not a prophet) scarcely stemmed the wall of dislike that eventually developed almost everywhere, with the possible exceptions of Japan, where he became somewhat of a celebrity intellectual late in life, and among Byzantine historians, who responded well to his later work on that subject. Ultimately, regardless of whether he rejected the title of prophet, Toynbee's work massively reduced respect for metahistory, most historians accepting Geyl's verdict that what he did was fundamentally antagonistic to what historians should do.

A handful of historians continued to give their approval, especially Herbert Butterfield. But even he noted Toynbee's appalling lack of understanding of science and his moralistic tone. More fundamentally, while endorsing his panoramic enterprise, Butterfield was privately critical of the a priori early planning of the study. However, he thought Toynbee's change of direction halfway through showed admirable flexibility. Butterfield, a believer in Providence, probably saw some similarities in Toynbee's increasingly spiritual emphasis.

Toynbee's broad canvas approach to history, his more secular observations in his earlier volumes of the *Study*, as well as his adversity theory undoubtedly helped in the establishment of present-day global/world history. But Michael Lang is probably correct in his assessment that, "to many world historians today, Arnold J. Toynbee is regarded like an embarrassing uncle at a house party."[42]

In 1963, Kenneth E. Bock made an interesting and somewhat overlooked observation in his review of Toynbee's last volume of the *Study*, in *History and Theory*:

> The basic objection to Toynbee's religious orientation ... appears to arise from his insistence that religion is not merely an element of civilization, not merely an institution that is to be taken into account in historical investigation, but that it is a distinct and independent phenomenon that gives history its only meaning. Since this is Toynbee's conviction, it follows that religious faith or spiritual insight or inspiration are basic tools in his work as a historian. To the extent that this is so, Toynbee speaks as prophet. I cannot see why Toynbee would conscientiously deny it. But what is involved in being a prophet? And what is a prophet? These are questions that his critics have not squarely faced.[43]

In 1989, on the centenary of Toynbee's birth, a group of historians under the direction of C.T. McIntire and Marvin Perry, undertook to reopen "critical consideration of Toynbee now that his work is complete, and of asking our colleagues in the academic world and the world of public affairs to think freshly about his extraordinary achievement." The volume, which was not an "attempt to examine his thought comprehensively,"[44] received mixed responses, and no massive reconsiderations of Toynbee's oeuvre followed.

Fairly recently in *History and Theory*, a number of historians once again raised the issues of the responsibilities of the historian, including the parameters of the discipline as well as the wall of separation between history and the study of religion, but this discussion included scarcely a reference to Toynbee.[45]

While Toynbee's endeavours may never be fully re-examined – and with some justification, given the inadequacies of his methodology and the controversy over the role he finally assigned to himself – there remains a gaping hole in the work of professional historians in the quest for meaning in history. I think it is worth at least some soul searching before turning such concerns completely over to other disciplines.

Yuval Noah Harari: History without Meaning

Yuval Noah Harari is a remarkable historian. Although he is a comparatively young scholar, his works have already had a major impact upon both academia and the wider world of history lovers beyond the academy. In contrast, figures such as Acton and Toynbee took almost a lifetime to achieve such fame. Harari's accomplishment is especially remarkable, as it is in the field of global history, an area where theorizing, beyond the level of textbook surveys, has been virtually a taboo area for most historians since the last, sad days of Arnold J. Toynbee. When I say Harari's works, I mean *Sapiens: A Brief History of Humankind* (English translation, 2014), an international bestseller, and *Homo Deus: A Brief History of Tomorrow* (English translation, 2016), well on its way to becoming the same. A professor of history at the Hebrew University of Jerusalem, he has also published in the field of medieval and renaissance military history, his original subject of research while obtaining his DPhil at Oxford.

While the prospect inhibits many academics, who in any case prefer to be topic introverts, there has been a move towards analysing broad patterns in history by both a handful of university historians and a much larger group outside the ivory towers. The "big history" concept has gained quite a following, especially after a television documentary by that name aired in 2013. David Christian is somewhat of a celebrity figure in this genre as is Jared Diamond of *Guns, Germs and Steel* (1999) fame, the latter being acknowledged by Harari as an inspiration to him. Nevertheless, macro-historical processes, which Harari teaches, are still a novelty area in the history departments of most universities.

In this section I wish to discuss the arguments presented in *Sapiens* and *Homo Deus* together, though the last book is, strictly speaking, about the future. In my view, examining these books together affords the best opportunity for understanding Harari's concept of the forces at play in shaping our world as a sort of continuum inextricably linking past, present, and future. A continuum is in keeping with his view of history. According to Harari, there is nothing preordained in history. Rather like in our everyday experience, things simply happen by chance and cannot be predicted (i.e., level two chaos).[46] As he states in *Sapiens*, "We study history not to know the future but to widen our horizons, to understand that our present situation is neither natural nor inevitable and that we consequently have many more possibilities before us than we imagine."[47] He essentially repeats this declaration in *Homo Deus*: "Historians study the past not in order to repeat it, but in order to be liberated from it ... Studying history aims to loosen the grip of the past."[48]

I should also state early and clearly that Harari takes a completely materialistic view of what we are. We are a species of animals. The key to our happiness is how we manipulate the biochemical system. As he states:

> As far as we can tell, from a purely scientific viewpoint, human life has no meaning. Humans are the outcome of blind evolutionary processes that operate without goal or purpose. Our actions are not part of some divine cosmic plan, and if planet Earth were to blow up tomorrow morning,

the universe would probably keep going about its business as usual. As far as we can tell at this point, human subjectivity would not be missed. Hence any meaning that people ascribe to their lives is just a delusion.[49]

But delusion can be powerful, and has been throughout the history of sapiens.

The power of delusion has to do with the very nature of Homo sapiens. According to the narrative in *Sapiens*, our species of animal emerged from a chain of developments in Africa about 200,000 years ago. About 70,000 years ago, "history" began with the so-called Cognitive Revolution. At that time, Homo sapiens began displaying an ability to transmit information – through gossip, for example – beyond the skills of other, more archaic humans such as Neanderthals. But their most distinctive characteristic was their ability to share ideas about things that did not exist, in fictive language. This ability to creatively imagine, Harari argues, allowed Homo sapiens to migrate and, by 13,000 years ago, to become the exclusive species of the genus Homo.

What followed in the next thousand years was the establishment of permanent settlements based on the domestication of plants and animals, known as the Agricultural Revolution. This allowed for a massive expansion in population in the centuries that followed. Was it a happy development? Certainly not for the livestock, our fellow animals, who were subjected to routine cruelty. Did it make us happier than had we continued our lives as hunter-foragers? Probably not. So why did people make the "wheat bargain"? Harari's answer is that it was for "the same reason that people throughout history have miscalculated. People were unable to fathom the full consequences of their decisions."[50] Thus, in one of his most controversial assessments, Harari states, "The Agricultural Revolution was history's biggest fraud."[51] For Harari, "no matter what you call it – game theory, postmodernism or memetics – the dynamics of history are not directed toward enhancing human well-being."[52] This idea departs sharply from the usual narrative in most world history textbooks of a string of achievements, with the Agricultural Revolution as perhaps the turning point.

Finally, according to Harari, about 500 years ago, the Scientific Revolution – the third great revolution in the status of Homo sapiens – commenced. The result is that sapiens today dominates the entire global environment, unifying the planet with an ongoing geopolitical order; economic, legal, and scientific systems; and religious conglomerates. While Harari believes in no overall meaning to history, he does see it as having a direction. If we adopt "the viewpoint of a cosmic spy satellite, which scans millennia rather than centuries. From such a vantage point it becomes crystal clear that history is moving relentlessly toward unity."[53]

This assertion brings us to the argument conveyed towards the end of *Sapiens* into *Homo Deus*: "Though the details are ... obscure, we can nevertheless be sure about the general direction of history. In the twenty-first century, the third big project of humankind will be to acquire for us divine powers of creation and destruction, and upgrade *Homo sapiens* into *Homo deus*."[54] Thus, he adds, "We may well think of the new human agenda as consisting really of only one project (with many branches): attaining divinity." Divinity, according to Harari, "isn't a vague metaphysical quality. And it isn't the same as omnipotence. When speaking of upgrading humans into gods, think more in terms of Greek gods or Hindu devas rather than the omnipotent biblical sky father."[55] Thus, in the latter part of his first book and throughout his second, Harari identifies the last and most significant observable trend in the ongoing narrative of Homo sapiens that comes the closest to seeing a meaning to history. But more of this later. I would like, first, to consider Harari's work within the context of morality.

Harari is again quite clear in his view of the exclusively material nature of humankind: "Scientists studying the inner workings of the human organism have found no soul there. They increasingly argue that human behavior is determined by hormones, genes and synapses, rather than by free will – the same forces that determine the behavior of chimpanzees, wolves and ants."[56] Yet he does see through most of sapiens history that it has been governed by securing rules of morality, not always the same, but nevertheless operational. He links this quest to religion, one of the great unifiers of humankind and sources of social stability. As he states, "*Religion* can thus be defined as a system of *human norms and values that is founded on a belief in a supernatural order*." It involves two distinct criteria: first, "religions hold that there is a supernatural order which is not the product of human whims or agreement"; and, second, "based on this superhuman order, religion establishes norms and values that it considers binding."[57] Further, Harari states that religion "gives a complete description of the world, and offers a well-defined contract with predetermined goals."[58] He insists that religions should not be confused with spirituality: the latter is "a dangerous threat," often ending in disruptions in the religion and the society, as with, for example, "the spiritual truth-seekers" who started the Protestant Reformation.[59]

Harari observes that monotheism, as opposed to polytheism, has also generally prevailed in the modern world. Dualistic religions, such as Zoroastrianism, have disappeared along the road, although they explained evil in a clearer way than did monotheism. Monotheism, with its emphasis on unity, has been less tolerant with dissidents. As he notes, "More Christians were killed by fellow Christians" during the twenty-four hours of the St. Bartholomew's Day Massacre in 1572 "than by the polytheistic Roman Empire throughout its entire existence."[60]

While religion asserted that all humans were subject to a system of moral laws that "we did not invent and that we cannot change," it did not always entail a belief in god(s). In contrast to the Abrahamic religions, for example, "other religions, from Buddhism and Daoism to Nazism, communism and liberalism, argue that superhuman laws are natural laws, and not the creation of this or that god. Of course, each believes in a different set of natural laws discovered and revealed by different seers and prophets, from Buddha and Laozie to Hitler and Lenin."[61] Under this wide definition of religion, capitalism, for example, evolved into a religion. It began as a set of ideas about the economy but became increasingly "both descriptive and prescriptive," transforming itself into an ethic – "a set of teachings about how people should behave, educate their children and even think." He adds, "This new religion has had a decisive influence on the development of modern science, too."[62]

In modern times, "the uncompromising quest for truth is a spiritual journey, which can seldom remain within the confines of either religious or scientific establishments," for each upholds different truths and has different interests – religion "above all in order," and science "above all in power." Religions once supplied "the cosmic plan" that "gave meaning to human life."[63] In due course, modern culture rejected this belief.

Just as the Agricultural Revolution "gave rise to theist religions, the Scientific Revolution gave birth to humanist religions in which humans replaced gods."[64] As Harari states, "The greatest scientific discovery was the discovery of ignorance. Once humans realized how little they knew about the world, they suddenly had very good reason to seek new knowledge, which opened up the scientific road to progress."[65] He sees humanism triumphing in this situation but, like every successful religion, ultimately fragmenting into conflicting sects – orthodox, socialist, and evolutionary. Liberalism became the humanists' creed, with its emphasis on free choice as the ultimate authority. However, the theory of evolution denied not only eternal souls but ultimately the concept of free will. The latter idea has been very difficult for liberalism, which maintains that "each individual voter, customer and viewer ought to use his or her free will in order to create meaning not just for his or her life, but for the entire universe."[66]

The idea of free will had supplied a meaning to life in modern times, but "the life sciences undermine liberalism, arguing that the free individual is just a fictional tale concocted by an assembly of biochemical algorithms."[67] This disavowal has been hard to take, even for New Atheist such as Richard Dawkins and Steven Pinker, "champions of the new scientific world view," who refuse to abandon liberalism.[68] Yet, argues Harari, the "great decoupling" of science and liberal philosophy has begun. "The new projects of the twenty-first century – gaining immortality, bliss and divinity" – will try to serve all of humankind, but the probable result may be "the creation of a new superhuman caste that will abandon its liberal roots and treat normal humans no better than nineteenth-century Europeans treated Africans."[69] New religions will emerge from research laboratories, culminating in "data religion" that will claim to determine right and wrong in the name of the freedom of information. In the process, Homo sapiens will vanish, upgraded into a new species, Homo deus.[70] Thus, perhaps a tale of progress and/or meaning in history could be attempted by reading back from the establishment of the Internet-of-All-Things and the vanishing of Homo sapiens in a reconstruction of human history through four stages beginning with the Cognitive Revolution.[71] But, for Harari, none of this is preordained or prophecy.

Much of what Harari says is fascinating, tinged at times with sensationalism. It might be possible for a subject specialist to discover some factual error or common misconceptions. But this could be said of any broad study or world history textbook – or *any* serious work of history for that matter. On the whole, Harari's references seem to reflect up-to-date scholarship. As stated earlier, he does not get into the debate over historical facts as truth. But it is clear that he seeks truth. His view of the Agricultural Revolution, like that of Jared Diamond, is eccentric, based in part on his own "moral" outrage over the treatment of animals (he is a vegetarian), and has had its share of critics, even from one reviewer and overall fan – Bill Gates! However, like much of what he says, it has an honest quality.

His bias against monotheistic religions is also evident in many places. Unfortunately for Harari, his honesty has provided some possible counter-arguments, especially from theists. He states in *Sapiens* that "history proceeds from one junction to the next, choosing for some mysterious reason to follow first this path, then another."[72] He provides many examples of this "mysterious reason" at key transitional stages in the history of sapiens. At the beginning, he asks, "What ... drove forward the evolution of the massive human brain during those two million years?" and answers, "Frankly, we don't know."[73] During the appearance of new ways of thinking and communicating between 70,000 to 30,000 years ago (the Cognitive Revolution), "Why did it occur in Sapiens DNA rather than that of Neanderthals? It was a matter of pure chance, as far as we can tell."[74] Added to this honest statement is another question one might pose: How exactly did the members of sapiens convince each other of "the imagined reality of gods," and later of nations, and corporations, and human rights. This "imagined reality" has been so important down to the present, avoiding the charge of lying, and exhibiting the ability to change rapidly, for example, from the myth of the divine right of kings to the myth of sovereignty of the people in the French Revolution. The secret, according to Harari, is that it "probably" began with the appearance of fiction.[75] He asks similar questions about the Scientific Revolution. Why did it begin in western Europe rather than in China or India, and why at the midpoint of the second millennium BCE? Harari's answer, "We don't know – scholars have proposed dozens of theories, but none of them is particularly convincing."[76]

Toynbee had his adversity theory, or challenge and response, as one possible kick-start mechanism for civilizations. Harari really has none. Could not some plausible argument be introduced here in the form of Divine Providence? It seems incredible that a species is repeatedly so successful in reproducing its DNA through the ages and becoming dominant not only over the earth, but potentially over a universe. Going through each of these phases in its history, could its success have been the product of sheer accident and coincidence? Is there no pattern of progress so overwhelming as to suggest a meaning to history? In contradiction to Harari's acceptance of the important role of accident, there are certainly statements about the last stage in the narrative of sapiens where he speaks of the process of moving towards unity as "irreversible."[77]

There is also the realm of imagination, so important in leading sapiens to dominion over the planet. Where did it come from? Is it not kindred to the spirituality referred to by Harari as a force driving people to demand change, as in the truth seekers of the Protestant Reformation.[78] Surely it is a component in the formation not only of actual religions but of the quasi- or secular religions and ideologies through the ages.

In the final scenario envisaged by Harari – the demise of Homo sapiens and the birth of Homo deus – is there not something repulsive to most readers? Does it not evoke something of the feelings of readers of dystopian novels? It both degrades humanity and does not end well. With respect to the version of evolutionary (or scientific) humanism devised by Julian Huxley in the early twentieth century (which was reasonably successful for a time in attracting some liberal humanist scientists as a secular religion), surely part of its failure was due to its founder's unquestioned adherence to eugenics as well as the assumption of godly status by an intellectual elite over the rest of humanity. In the last resolve, doesn't God seem a better choice? But then again Harari himself admits the possibility of a final sunset for sapiens that is not a happy fate for the bulk of the species. As he has stated for earlier transitions, "the dynamics of history are not directed toward enhancing human well-being."[79] He sees his job as presenting truthful observations, not perpetually enkindling delusion and false hopes.

Towards a Contemporary Theist View of History

It now seems appropriate to present a theist view of history alongside that of the materialist interpretation of Harari. Toynbee, in the opinion of some, presented such a view but in an idiosyncratic way and only at certain stages of his work. Regrettably, it must be supplied here in the form of a proposal or outline rather than a detailed, full study from antiquity to the present. It is also necessary to make the additional admission that this theist view cannot match the clean lines of argumentation and expression found in *Homo Sapiens* and *Homo Deus*.

In these two master works, Harari unfolds a consistently materialist narrative unequivocally denying any supernatural agency in history. Human beings are animals, possess no souls, and live lives that are individually and collectively meaningless in the traditional sense of the term. Materialism precludes meaning, although it may not preclude patterns of behaviour that seem of considerable duration to contemporaries in any given period of history, but in the long haul of the ages are short term. At the other end of the spectrum, my job is to present a theist view that purports to contain a great deal of meaning. However, in order to present the sources of this view, I must concede that any attempt to synthesize the views of even the largest of world religions could become very messy. Here, I will therefore attempt to present a theist overview informed by more specific traditions that have affected my own life.

My background, as I indicated in the introduction, is that of a Catholic Christian. In theology, I am liberal; in social outlook, a Social Christian in the tradition of the Anglican archbishop William Temple and the Roman Catholic layperson Barbara Ward. I have limited acquaintance with the great Eastern religions such as Hinduism and even those faiths that are within the Abrahamic family – Judaism and Islam. That such a synthesis of world religions is possible, I have no doubt – for example, someone who has displayed that ability is Robert Wright, a secular humanist, in his book *The Evolution of God* (2009). Beyond Catholicism, I do possess considerable knowledge of the other branches of Christianity through personal experience and academic study. So the title of this section could more justifiably read "Towards a Contemporary *Christian* View of History."

I would make the initial observation that Harari's scholarship is obviously better informed by modern science than that of Toynbee. Acceptance of the Darwinian framework of evolution is an integral part of his tale of humankind. This acceptance would immediately contrast with the historical views of some Christian evangelicals who adhere to a strict fundamentalist interpretation of the Bible on the origins and early history of humankind. They would not accept the basic findings of Charles Darwin. While perhaps discounting the seventeenth-century calculation of Archbishop Ussher concerning the creation of the earth in 4004 BCE and recognizing the scant evidence of such events as the Great Flood, they would essentially follow the arguments of William Paley in *Natural Theology* (1802), that God the Creator was like a divine watchmaker, placing all elements of the earth in careful harmony through the special creation of each species of plant and animal.

The scientific-historical position of these fundamentalist Christians developed in the nineteenth century. While works as early as Robert Chambers's *Vestiges of Creation* (1841) introduced the idea of a series of developmental stages in the chronology of nature, it was still linked to God's superintendence. But nothing then or now equalled the outcry against Charles Darwin's *On the Origin of Species*, first published in 1859. The theory of evolution through natural selection clashed directly with the Bible's version of creation. In 1871, the place of humankind in Darwin's account was made even more explicit with the publication of his *The Descent of Man*. Even before this second book, a small army of non-believers led by Darwin's friend Thomas Huxley (credited with the invention of the word "agnostic") had linked their cause with that of "science." The famous debate between Huxley, "Darwin's bulldog," and Bishop Samuel Wilberforce, an early opponent of the theory of evolution, at the British Association for the Advancement of Science meeting at Oxford in 1860 set the pattern for a huge clash between religion and science in the ensuing decades.

Not all prominent scientists in this period readily embraced Darwinism. Indeed, Huxley himself had some misgivings about Darwin's theory of natural selection, and a majority of evolutionists probably did not believe in random variation. But vulgarized versions of Darwin's ideas prevailed through the efforts of agnostics and atheists such as the former tinsmith and leader of the secularist movement George Jacob Holyoake. On the other hand, James R. Moore, in *The Post Darwinian Controversies* (1979), has warned modern readers not to overstress the warfare between religion and science, pointing to the existence of many Christian Darwinists who were committed to peace between the positions. In the same vein, Charles Taylor, in *A Secular Age* (2007), has warned us not to overemphasize the causal role of science in today's irreligion.

Although a reconciliation of sorts with evolution began to prevail in the ranks of mainstream Protestant churches by the early twentieth century, the 1925 Scopes "monkey trial" in the "Bible belt" of the southern United States was a reminder of the continuing tension. Sir Julian Huxley, T.H. Huxley's grandson, later unleashed a new wave of conflict with his 1959 address "The Evolutionary Vision" delivered at the University of Chicago's Darwin Centennial Conference. Huxley's well-publicized line that "the evolutionary man can no longer take refuge from his loneliness in the arms of a divinized father-figure whom he has himself created" may well have been a prime catalyst for the modern wave of creationism in reaction to it.

Roman Catholicism, in contrast, had been much less hostile to Darwin's theories. Possibly as a result of the scientific work of Jean-Baptiste Lamarck and Gregor Mendel, both Catholics, the idea of development through nature did not hit an early, solid wall of opposition. Development or evolution through the overall agency and superintendence of God seemed reasonable, assisted by a less literal interpretation of the Bible, the latter not being the only source of traditional beliefs for Catholics.

Thus, no huge obstacle existed for liberal Protestants and Roman Catholics in the acceptance of a framework for a narrative of human history supplied by anthropologists and archaeologists working under the assumptions of general evolutionary theory. What would be unacceptable were further assumptions about a rudderless, meaningless saga of Homo sapiens as depicted by Harari.

In the historical narrative of liberal Protestants and Catholics, there was a chain of triumphs and achievements from the emerging dominance of Homo sapiens over other species, from the Agrarian Revolution to the Scientific Revolution to the present. For such believers, Divine Providence had a hand in this chain of development, of course. For the general public in a more secular environment, this narrative was also a purposeful success story. In other words, the Judeo-Christian notion of linear progress through history could live, for the most part, with the linear, progressive view of liberal rationalists, as was evidenced in most college "civ" textbooks.

The telos or final outcome of history was clear to most Christians in the ultimate meaning of life – union with God. But the length of this period before the union in actual time was unclear. The belief of many early Christians was that the Second Coming was imminent. Today, most believe that it will be in the distant future. Such speculation has resulted in all kinds of variations of the Second Coming, including identifying the "signs" of the end through the Book of Revelation, specific preachings of many Evangelicals, and the beliefs of Doomesday cults, especially in faith-based popular history on television mentioned in Chapter 4.

In a much more significant way, in the case of Social Christians, from the early Anglican founders of English Christian socialism in the nineteenth century such as F.D. Maurice, the Incarnation placed God in literal fatherhood over human society, linked to the brotherhood of humanity. The coming of the Second Adam (Jesus) necessitated social compassion and unity within society. Subsequent Social Christians of most denominations therefore believed that the Kingdom of God was in a sense already at hand and one must initiate immediate social action to improve society.[80]

For Christopher Dawson, a Roman Catholic cultural historian, the Incarnation signalled the mixing of the eternal with ordinary time, giving history not only a direction but clearly indicating Divine intervention in the life of mankind by direct action at certain points in history.[81] This renewed concept of Providence was viewed as part of the coordination of the divine and human, the City of God with the City of Man (in the terminology of St. Augustine). As Dawson states, "the religious instinct finds its fullest and most concrete satisfaction in the historical field – through faith in an historical person, an historical community, and an historical tradition."[82]

Barbara Ward, an economist and champion of the developing world and the celebrated author of *The Rich Nations and the Poor Nations* (1961), had a close association with Dawson in the Sword of the Spirit movement during the Second World War. She certainly took a position similar to Dawson on the Incarnation, seeing it as "the supreme intervention of God in time." She also saw that Christianity "was a religion of the spirit but it was not one that rejected the world as illusion." In her view, Christianity had an edge over Hinduism and Buddhism in this respect. Her ultimate hope was that all great world religions would come into union with the Ground Source of all Reality. Historically, she believed Christianity to be "the flowering" of Judaism and Greek thought.[83] In the mid-twentieth century she parted with Dawson on the question of Western culture, taking a much more positive view of liberalism. She saw liberty growing out of a common heritage with Christianity.[84]

As a leading advocate of Social Catholicism and ecumenism, Ward advanced the cause of Social Christianity from Europe and North America and into the developing world. She was also a pioneer in the field of environmentalism, linking it strongly to her religious beliefs. As she argued in *Faith and Freedom* in 1954, "This God of the Jews was not a nature god. He was something more. He was the God of nature ... Nature's Cause and Creator." She believed firmly that, in Christian teaching, humankind "is called by God to be a co-creator in building a more reliable, useful and indeed beautiful world."[85] Thus Ward invited a theist interpretation of history that is environmental and global and very much in interaction with the real world.

Both Barbara Ward and Christopher Dawson would agree that Christianity is deeply embedded in Western culture. Whether Western culture could survive a completely post-Christian environment is an open question. The interactions between the great religious cultures of the globe concerning the meaning of history obviously deserve much more attention without drifting into the prophetic side of Toynbee's writings.

Concerning the questions of truth and morality, there is obviously much more that could be said from the theist (Christian) viewpoint. In relation to technical or secular history, as we have seen, it has much to offer beyond the realm of ecclesiastical "religious" history where Christian scholars have produced works of great scholarship. Christian theological concepts can explain the onward motion of progress beyond short-term triggers such as agricultural surpluses and adversity theory. But significant divisions exist as well. As we have seen, one is in the question of Creation. Another is what weight to place on social compassion (and thereby social sin) as emphasized by Social Christianity, and the lingering but widespread belief in original sin still found in the official theology of both conservative Protestants and Catholics.

Original sin certainly explains much of the evil tendencies in humankind as well as the free will we have to choose the evil over the good path regardless of some sort of Providence in operation. Traditionally, many Christians have believed that the moral system, the rock bed of behaviour, is innate, part of our very nature. As such, it is part of natural law – a concept stretching back to Greco-Roman thought. It has even had a bearing on the "moral zeitgeist" (thanks to memes) believed in by New Atheists such as

Richard Dawkins and Sam Harris. It was earlier employed by C.S. Lewis in *Mere Christianity* (1952) as proof that its existence in all humanity leads us, in turn, to proof of the existence of a Divine architect.

A few years ago, most Christians would probably have accepted the views of Lord Acton or Goldwin Smith that the content of moral laws remains unchanged by time and culture. But more recent theology has questioned this and questioned whether natural law is unchanging. By the 1960s, the old view came to be known as "classicism" by some Christian theologians. It began to be replaced by "historical consciousness," which, in the view of Charles Davis (and Bernard Lonergan), "sees man as a person or subject in the process of becoming. Man's being is a becoming for which he is responsible, and community as properly human is made by his freedom." Truth, in other words, is not "static," as the Greeks and the early church would have seen it, but "dynamic" and must be "looked for in its historical setting."[86]

Such a position is traceable at least to John Henry Newman's concepts in his *Essay on the Development of Christian Doctrine* (1845), where he tried to present his ideas on the development of theological doctrine for an orderly theological process forward by his colleagues. It was updated in the mid-twentieth century by the Jesuit Karl Rahner. It was not meant to go so far as some religious liberals would take it. It was not meant, as Martin D'Arcy has described it, to move to the position of the historical relativists: "History without realizing the fact was intent on murdering its own claims to truth."[87] Historians do not inhabit quite the same realm as theologians.

For Catholics in the history business, all of this would indicate that the old belief in immutable truth could be modified into a concept of core beliefs derived from Revelation, surrounded by other truths subject to the changing circumstances of time and place. Some truths are more central than others. Moreover, truth is not neatly bundled into one system but is more a series of fragments to be connected together.

The impact of such ideas on the concept of truth in history for Christians is obvious. Have they any immediate implications for moral judgments in history? We have seen that many professional historians of Christian background, such as Dom David Knowles, Regius Professor of Modern History at Cambridge (1954–63), had firmly rejected the role of the historian as moral judge. Viewing truth in a less rigid way, on the other hand, for some might be the path to moral relativism as much as historical relativism. If such an approach shifted a little more towards more neutrality on the outrages of the past, it could actually disgust New Atheists such as Sam Harris as much as many Christians. This situation creates yet a few additional problems in the creation of a technical piece of history acceptable to a broad spectrum of readers.

I would be remiss in my duty to discuss the Christian perspective if I did not mention Eastern Orthodoxy. Its roots, like those of Roman Catholicism, go back to the early fathers of the church and a shared legacy of doctrinal development through the first seven Ecumenical Councils until the separation of the two churches in the eleventh century. Since that time, Eastern Orthodoxy has expanded from essentially the Greek church of the Byzantine Empire into a group of self-governing autocephalous national churches with the ecumenical Patriarchate of Constantinople as the first among equals, a largely honorary position. The Western Catholic Church continued to be governed by the pope of Rome, whose primacy in the form of dogmatic and jurisdictional authority remained supreme.

The different Orthodox churches have a less agreed doctrinal uniformity, with non-dogmatic teaching varying among them. They have experienced much oppression since the fall of the Byzantine Empire, especially in the Balkans until the nineteenth century. But they have helped to define national identity in the strongest possible terms in places like Serbia and Bulgaria, not to mention in Greece. Within Orthodoxy, there has always been a strong leaning towards mysticism that would know no national borders.

The Russian Orthodox Church, by far the largest in Eastern Orthodoxy, has had its schisms within the fold and had an often complicated relationship with the tsarist state. In the twentieth century, it endured severe repression during the early days of the Communist regime under Stalin. This changed somewhat in the Second World War, when the dictator tried to use it as a propaganda tool during the "Patriotic War" against the Nazis. After the fall of communism, it has experienced a remarkable revival, but still a rather complicated relationship persists with the state. Within the Russian church, what has often been a comfort to the people besides mysticism is *sobornost* – the notion of spiritual community involving cooperation against pronounced individualism. One of the great lay theologians of the nineteenth century, Vladimir Solovev (1853–1900), tried to develop the concept in a way that would produce a fusion of many competing ideologies of his age. Nicholas Berdyaev (1874–1948), also a theological philosopher within the Orthodox tradition, engaged in more direct confrontation with a host of ideologies including liberal rationalism. An opponent of anything that inhibited creativity, he also had a mystic quality. His historical writings contributed much to the understanding of the concept of Moscow as the Third Rome. Eastern Orthodoxy deserves more attention with respect to the attitude of its leaders and theologians on the issues of truth, morality, and meaning in history.

One last observation must be made in relation to the Christian view of history. Since the Enlightenment, the role of Christianity in history has received its share of criticism in the Western world. Certainly, the behaviour of the Western church in the Early and High Middle Ages has often been linked with pretentions of papal monarchy, suppression of dissent, intolerance, and crusades of aggression, with the intrigues of Byzantium not faring much better. This narrative has co-existed with the view of others that the church saved the best of the culture of the classical world of Rome and Greece after the collapse of the Roman Empire, fostering a rebirth in higher education in the High Middle Ages to the Renaissance. The Reformation and the seventeenth-century Wars of Religion have seen their share of sharp criticisms from various viewpoints of the various sides. The Scientific Revolution and the Enlightenment have formed a narrative of the downward path of religious dominance into the twentieth century in much secular history writing.

Christianity has also received its share of sympathetic historians showing its positive contributions to moral and social improvements, from the abolition of slavery to more compassionate care of the poor. In the course of the past century and a half in Britain and North America, we have seen the production of sound works of historical scholarship taking a positive view of the roles of Christianity into modern times. Although many of these historians have resided in Religious Studies Departments, others have been in the secular mainstream of what Butterfield would call technical history.

Unfortunately, the newest grand narratives such as those by Harari have indicated a hostility towards the role of religion – in his case, monotheistic ones in particular. New Atheists such as Richard Dawkins, when they engage in the construction of any kind of historical narratives within their writings, tend to discredit traditional religion, refusing to assign it any positive role in the advancement of moral progress. The most extreme example of this would be *God Is Not Great: How Religion Poisons Everything* (2007) by the late Christopher Hitchens.

The reconciliation of these views with those of theists will not be an easy task. Even within the history of one country, faced with roughly the same body of evidence, it would be difficult, but not impossible, to strike a narrative path acceptable to most, as illustrated very recently in *American Covenant: A History of Civil Religion from the Puritans to the Present* (2017) by Philip S. Gorski. In that book, Gorski outlines three different historical visions operating within the United States – those of a Christian nation, a secular democracy, and a combination of the two. Nevertheless, such efforts could achieve better results than hostile positions argued from a priori assumptions, as in the case of Hitchens, or in opposition to a theist narrative, in the case of Harari.

Why Seek Meaning?

For most historians teaching, reading, and writing in their specific fields of investigation, the search for meaning or an overall pattern to history has not been a professional priority. Indeed, very few have engaged in it and many of their colleagues have probably been suspicious of those who did. It can involve the importation of concepts outside the discipline, which for some is ultra vires. One does not have to be a rigid positivist to feel that the objectivity of empirical research could be compromised in the pursuit of some a priori goal or assumption rooted in some sort of secular, theological, or philosophical ideology.

Today, the few historians who engage in such a pursuit do so at their own risk, frequently being viewed as dilettantes or amateurs or worse. Some pursue it professionally under the protective cover of historiography or outside the discipline as philosophers of history, anthropologists/sociologists, or literary and language authorities. In other cases, the potentially lucrative production of surveys of Western and/or world history, demanded by college students and the public, has made potential authors face the necessity of tracing some sort of central thread or organizing principle in all history, as noted by Geoffrey Barraclough.[88] Such an exercise has most often led to narratives heralding the advancement of humanity through the ages, ending in the triumph of worthwhile ideals and material achievements. Even Providence continues to be a viable hypothesis through the works of Herbert Butterfield, Christopher Dawson, and others, though they are circulated less and less.

Many of those who read history seem to seek some sort of hope with respect to the fate of humanity. If positive paths are not in evidence, the alternative can be despair. For such readers, perhaps the ultimate danger to be avoided is a pointless saga with happenings governed by chance. Yet Yuval Noah Harari has successfully emerged with a somewhat different solution – embrace the uncertainty! After all, something unanticipated could still appear to maintain current trends and allow the species some hope of survival in its present form.

Suggested Readings

Herbert Butterfield, *Christianity and History* (London: G. Bell and Sons, 1949)

Christopher Dawson, *Progress and Religion: An Historical Enquiry* (London: Sheed and Ward, 1929)

Mircea Eliade, *The Myth of the Eternal Return or, Cosmos and History* (Princeton, NJ: Princeton University Press, 1971)

C.T. McIntire, *Herbert Butterfield: Historian as Dissenter* New Haven, CT: Yale University Press, 2004)

C.T. McIntire and Marvin Perry, eds, *Toynbee: Reappraisals* (Toronto: University of Toronto Press, 1989)

William H. McNeill, *Arnold J. Toynbee: A Life* (New York: Oxford University Press, 1989)

R.I. Moore, "World History," *Companion to Historiography*, edited by Michael Bentley, 941–59 (London: Routledge, 1997)

Oswald Spengler, *The Decline of the West* (New York: Random House, 1965)

Charles Taylor, *A Secular Age* (Cambridge MA: Belknap Press of Harvard University Press, 2007) chapter four

History beyond the Academy

What has been written thus far in this book has been directed mainly at the academy – academic historians and their students. This is perhaps understandable, given my background. But what of the writers and readers beyond the universities? What about this world of enthusiastic activity, which currently has been experiencing an expansive, almost "boom," period? Where do the writers and producers of non-academic history books and other products stand on the issues of truth, morality, and meaning in history? A comparison is worth making between those works produced in this freer atmosphere governed largely by the demands for their products and those produced within the institutional pressures of academia, which tend to be limited to highly specialized books and learned journal articles for the purposes of the historian's own internal discipline. Given the vastness of this canvas, I have attempted to select areas of activity that, in my view, are most significant and provide some perspective. It is far from a complete picture.

Background

It is good to reflect upon the fact that the history business, if you will, was a thriving concern before the founding of schools and departments of history at universities, and it continues to be so to this day. Historical writing was available in the period of rising literacy in the early nineteenth century. By the mid-nineteenth century a pantheon of writers in almost every major country of the Western world soon supplied the needs of a growing audience. The purpose of these works was to inform as well as to entertain, the latter a goal often forgotten by professional academics. The barrier between fiction and non-fiction was respected but not one to be treated as almost a war zone. These writers focused on the great deeds and events of their individual countries as well as Western civilization as a whole. Usually concerned with the political elite, especially leaders, their motives and the results of their actions, such works frequently resulted in better defining national identities. There were a few exceptions to this trend: Jules Michelet (1798–1874), for example, tried to encompass France's history as the saga of a whole people in his *Histoire de France*, which appeared in many volumes in 1867. Even more specifically on the progress of the people was the work of John Richard Green (1837–1883) in his *A Short History of the English People* (1874). In Britain, readers were blessed with an unusually large number of gifted writer-historians in the nineteenth century, including Thomas Carlyle, Henry Hallam, John Lingard, J.A. Froude, E.A. Freeman, Samuel Rawson Gardiner, and, above all, Thomas Babington Macaulay.

Although all of these writers wrote from the perspective of their particular and varied political, religious, and social backgrounds and outlooks, they both entertained and helped to define the British nation. Not only did Macaulay receive a peerage for his efforts, but his five-volume *History of England* (1849–61) became an essential acquisition for the library of any respectable English individual. Well-educated in classics at university, Macaulay contributed to the *Edinburgh Review* and the *Encyclopedia Britannica*. A middle-of-the-road Whig-Liberal and moderate in religion, he saw his country steadily improving physically, intellectually, and morally.

Lord Acton, as a leader of the new academic discipline in Britain, thought little of these popular historians. He viewed Carlyle as "the most detestable of historians." For Acton, Carlyle's "doctrine of heroes, the doctrine that will is above law, comes next in atrocity to the doctrine that the flag covers the goods, and the cause justifies its agents, which is what Froude lives for."[1] As for Macaulay,

Acton wrote that his "essays are only pleasant reading, and a key to half the prejudices of our age ... He knew nothing respectably before the seventeenth century, he knew nothing of foreign history, of religion, of philosophy, science or art ... Read him therefore to find out how it comes that the most unsympathetic of critics can think him very nearly the greatest of English writers."[2] Acton's views on non-academic historians gained ground and, in time, were shared by many within the academy, some perhaps showing not-so-secret envy for their public success.

In North America, these names were also well known and were joined by American popular historians such as George Bancroft, William H. Prescott, and Francis Parkman. As in England, they were literary men to the core and shared the stage with historical fiction writers such as Sir Walter Scott, the latter being "by a wide margin, the most popular and imitated author in the early-nineteenth-century United States."[3] Even Ranke acknowledged that Scott had initially drawn him to the beauty of the past, although he kept that influence at a distance thereafter.

With the advent of the university-trained historian at the end of the nineteenth-century, many popular historians acknowledged the need for more thorough research. Peter Novick has also noted the purging of florid style in favour of a prose style more in keeping with "the moral posture of the historian."[4] Eventually this toned-down approach became evident even in those who had plied the trade for decades, not to mention a new generation of trained historians. But the tradition of the "potboilers" nevertheless persisted on the bookstands of the nation.

In Britain, informative and very well-written historical narratives have continued down to this day by non-academic authors such as Antonia Fraser. Historical fiction is also alive and well. In the United States, learned and readable accounts of a variety of subjects have been produced by private scholars such as David McCullough. Some, such as Alex Haley's *Roots*, have had unusually wide audience, enhanced by television adaptations. Haley's search for his own family's heritage had a major impact on race relations and the growth of Black history in the United States. In a similar way, the skilful stories of major events in Canadian history by the journalist Pierre Berton did much to advance the once-neglected field of Canadian history. Occasionally, history makers could be history writers, as with President Theodore Roosevelt in the United States and Prime Minister Winston Churchill in Great Britain.

Recently in Britain, a number of historians, such as Simon Schama, David Cannadine, and Niall Ferguson, have been able to attract large audiences with their works while retaining academic posts at home and abroad. A similar case can be found with Canadian author and academic Margaret MacMillan on the international stage and a number of historians in the field of Canadian history such as the late J.M. Bliss. Many such historians have built a secondary career on radio and/or television.

Multimedia

Historical documentaries were aired on both radio and television from the early days of these media. Popular experiments appeared on early "live" television, such as Walter Cronkite's *You Are There* (1953–7), which re-enacted important episodes in history with seeming engagement between narrator and prime participants. Television programs, usually on Sunday, often featured pastors using the Bible as a tool for understanding the religious past but also traversing into secular history, often with predictions of things to come. A contemporary program, *The Key of David*, uses Biblical passages, in this case Revelation 17:12–14, to reveal new insights on the Holy Roman Empire and its consequences down to the present. At the same time, a genre of archaeological programs has developed that argue against the historical accuracy of Biblical narratives. Examples of this are the *Bible's Buried Secrets* and the *Real Garden of Eden* on BBC-2, narrated by the Biblical scholar Francesca Stavrakopoulou.

By the late-1960s, a new aspect began to enter the picture in terms of the potential audience for history writers. As already mentioned, Alex Haley's *Roots* unleashed huge, popular interest in Black history beyond anything envisaged by academic writers. But much of this popularity was a product of the television adaptation – *Time* magazine pointed out that "half of all U.S. homes with a TV" watched the finale of that series. The same magazine also revealed that, while critics and scholars found fault with Haley's book, the basis of the series, such criticism did not seem to affect its popularity.[5]

Earlier, in 1969, Kenneth Clark's television series, *Civilization*, was launched. Not only was it a transatlantic success, in spite of some eccentricities on the part of the creator-narrator, it led to a host of imitators over the next two decades. Stepping out from behind-the-camera positions as consultants, some historians became media celebrities in their own right. In later years, this became true of Schama and Ferguson. David Starkey moved from academe to full-time work as a successful performer-narrator-creator of a number of television series on Tudor monarchs. On the North American side, Ken Burns created an acclaimed series on the US Civil War and followed it up with similar multi-episode documentaries on a range of different topics. Similarly, in Canada, CBC television produced and broadcast the seventeen-episode *Canada: A People's History* in 2000–1.

With the next wave of media expansion in cable television, the market for such programming expanded beyond the traditional television networks through vehicles such as the History Channel. Digitization of archival material also allowed for the first time widespread access to primary materials previously unavailable to the general public. Where the availability of pictorial records largely determined the type of topics presented on television, newly available online records such as census reports afford opportunities for research on all sorts of things on a much-expanded scale well beyond the stuff of television documentaries.

The online access to such material is "democratic" in the sense that it provides new areas for hands-on research by academic historians, university students at all levels, and so-called amateurs. In recent years, the new specialty of material history has developed at universities, which has greatly enlarged our understanding of the past. Combining the techniques of archaeology with digitized sources and traditional written archives material, it can provide a much clearer picture of the lives of ordinary people.[6] This interest in material history should be most welcome in activities that involve both academics and amateurs. Some of this interest was perhaps anticipated years ago in books such as *Victorian Things* (1988) by Asa Briggs.

In another area of history, the broader availability of resources has taken the exercise of tracing one's ancestry out of the hands of a small number of paid professionals. Genealogy is now a huge business, with companies supplying further verification using tools such as DNA services.

Never before has so much information been so available through the media. Paradoxically, there has been a concomitant rise of more fact-challenging opinions in the public arena, whether in arguments over global warming or televised political debates. Frequently politicians and journalists must employ "fact checkers" in such situations.

Another aspect of the new media is the creation of new kinds of publishing. Jack Doughtery and Kristen Nawrotzki's *Writing History in the Digital Age* (2013) involves, among other things, a re-visioning of historical writing (Part 1) through the spread of "publishing platforms."[7] The goal is not only to increase audiences through the digitization of conventional books but to change the ways in which books are produced, making them available through e-readers. This has become a huge blessing to writers, including academics, dealing with traditional presses that are hard pressed financially.

One step beyond e-readers is open access, with the Internet essentially becoming the publisher. It has had the negative effect of further weakening academic journals and publishing houses, especially university presses, which are criticized for their lack of cost efficacy, charging high prices while acting as "gatekeepers" for sound scholarship. Open access has encountered complications within the academy for the suggestion that such publications be taken as the equivalent of those that are normally published in prestigious journals and presses. Is the system of peer review compromised in an open-access system?

Together these situations can produce complex challenges and difficult decisions especially for young academics anxious to please their older, generally more traditional superiors. The inevitable deliberations by university rank and tenure committees can be very time consuming, and the decisions can often be quite damaging to a career, if proper agreements have not been worked out between faculty and heads of departments and the university administrations.

In terms of the central concerns of this book, such developments are neutral in their impact, other than consuming time that could be used in thinking about and discussing truth, morality, and meaning. Yet by reaching more people in a more accessible form, and in less time than conventional publishing, these developments can provide more opportunity for a wider audience to discuss the purposes of history. In the process, more readers and professional writers can be touched than ever before, and in an unrestricted manner. For the pure dissemination of knowledge, current approaches afford the opportunity to publish works that would not see the light of day because of their alleged lack of financial viability. The co-editors of *Writing History in the Digital Age* certainly concluded that publishing their volume in stages on the web "enriched its intellectual coherence and scope" beyond what might have been achieved through "traditional practices." They also concluded that "crowdsourcing" could improve writing and that the "wisdom of the crowd" played "an equal-or-greater-role in shaping our thinking as coeditors."[8]

Post-Truth

The events involving the US presidential election of 2016 have seen the rapid advance of distortion of facts in the media in the service of politics and of advocacy journalism, including hacking and cyber war. Where are the lines between the cherry picking of Wiki-Leaks, the claims of "fake news," and the unregulated stories abounding on social media? Small wonder that, at the end of

2016, the president of Oxford Dictionaries, Casper Grathwohl, had accepted a new word, "post-truth," defined as an adjective "relating to or denoting circumstances in which objective facts are less influential in shaping public opinion than appeals to emotional and personal belief."[9]

Lord Acton's boast that, as the archives of Europe were opened to all, historical truth would be made known to all seems so naive in today's world. Forms of counterfactual history have been around since the nineteenth century, of course. Sometimes called "hypothetical history," this genre essentially plays with contingency in exploring an important event in history by constructing an alternate scenario. In *If It Had Happened Otherwise* (1931), contributors produced essays on topics such as what would have followed had General Robert E. Lee won the Battle of Gettysburg. In many ways such efforts could be viewed as pointless.

The genre reappeared in a more serious historical and professional way over thirty years later with the publication of *Railways and American Economic Growth* (1964) by the economic historian Robert Fogel. Fogel attempted to understand the main forces generating the western expansion of the US economy by removing the role of railways and replacing it with a model of an expansion of the canal system. The objective was to assess the importance of railways as a factor in growth. Fogel's bold experiment was not taken up by a large number of academics interested in isolating causal factors in this way. However, in 1997 a very serious collection of essays appeared, edited by Niall Ferguson, entitled *Virtual History: Alternatives and Counterfactuals*. Ferguson, Robert Crowley, and William Thompson are among those who see hypothetical history as a useful technique in judging why certain factors should be emphasized more than others in assessing their role in important historical developments. It can also be stimulating for discussion purposes, be they in classrooms or on the Net. It does not challenge the truth of past events, developments, or accepted facts.

"Alternate history," on the other hand, is a genre of fiction not unlike literary fiction, science fiction, or historical fiction. It is not intended to serve the interests of academic history in the way in which counterfactual history claims to do. In an age of so many unregulated online communications, not only on websites but now in social media, including tweets, as well, have we not now entered a new realm in which the search for truth is no longer imperative, or at least is considered by some as co-equal with the use of "alternative facts" (i.e., falsehoods)? The latter term has come into use since the clash between Trump spokespersons and journalists since the inauguration of the new president in January 2017.

Yet we are reminded in the recent film *Denial* (2016) of the potential costs of such a situation. It was based on the libel suit brought against historian Deborah Lipstadt and her publisher, Penguin Books, by writer David Irving in 1996 for her published comments that Irving was a Holocaust denier. As the suit was brought to a British court, the burden of proof (i.e., that there was a Holocaust) was placed upon Lipstadt, played by Rachel Weisz. The trial, which entailed the calling of experts in the field and the presentation of evidence to establish the very well-knows facts of the Nazi policy of genocide in the Second World War, was surprisingly complicated, given the requirements of the UK court system. Although Lipstadt's vindication in 2000 was indeed a victory for history, the trial was a reminder that even well-known truths require constant defence.

The Power of Myth

To tie the notion of historical truth in such a way to what could be known at the time is surely disputable. One is inclined at least to say that if it was not yet true in 1492 that what Columbus discovered was America, it is certainly true now, and now is when the historian's judgement is being made.

William Dray, "Philosophy and Historiography"

At the core of all nations are sets of beliefs usually depicted as based on the historical experiences of those nations. Past events in wars, for example, are often seen as the turning points in the advance of peoples to full nationhood. Consider the case of the Serbs against Muslims in fourteenth-century Kosovo or the struggles of early Russians against the onslaught of Teutonic knights in roughly the same period in defining the soul of their modern nations. In a more recent and British constitutional context, one might consider how the events of the First World War led to more fully sovereign nationhood in the popular imagination of Canada and Australia.

And then there are the little sacred spots embedded in past histories. Michel-Rolph Trouillot has discussed a number of these in his book *Silencing the Past: Power and the Production of History* (1995). The subjects range from Columbus Day and the merchandizing of the Alamo, where the centrality of the event/person can be altered and re-created through the new needs of generations, to US slavery and the Holocaust, events that can become a central defining symbol of a nation through the ages; and to attempts to suppress the memory of events such as the Haitian Revolution (1791–1804). As Trouillot points out, debates about these subjects involve not only professional historians but politicians, journalists, activists promoting a particular interpretation, and the general public. As he argues, "Even in highly complex societies where the weight of the guild is significant, never does the historians' production constitute a closed corpus."[10] In such circumstances, while it is important for a path to be seen to truth, truth is often held to be something in service of an emotionally grounded patriotic faith. However, the recent wave of Confederate statue removals in the American South or of General Edward Cornwallis, founder of the city of Halifax, Nova Scotia reflected the increased sensitivity to the sufferings of racial minorities, past and present. Such instances provide an on-going corrective to the maintenance of entrenched positions of public mythology.

History as a Substitute for Religion

Margaret MacMillan, in her *The Uses and Abuses of History* (2008), has observed that, in our present-day world, "History with a capital H is being called in to fill the void" once occupied by traditional religion. History now "takes on the role of showing us good and evil, virtues and vices," given that religion "no longer plays as important a part as it once did in setting moral standards and transmitting values." For MacMillan, "History ... restores a sense, not necessarily of a divine being, but of something above and beyond human beings. It is our authority: It can vindicate us and judge us, and damn those who oppose us."[11]

The purpose of this section is not to supply a full critique of MacMillan's comment. Although the claim is stated rather boldly in her book, history as a substitute for religion is not much developed in her overall survey on the uses and abuses of history by various groups and causes. However, I found her observation to be intriguing and worthy of application, especially to the sprawling world of history beyond the academy. As MacMillan's belief is not that "History" (with a capital "H") is functioning precisely as a religion functions, I also feel the sociological ideas of Weber, Durkheim, and others on religion do not need formal review and application to this situation. However, I will test the statements by MacMillan first in a spirit of affirmation and then take a contrarian view on points where it seems the proposition does not work.

Long before the "history craze" of the present, at least one important thinker in the Western world feared what MacMillan believes is now taking place. Cardinal Newman, in *The Idea of a University* (1858), stated the following:

> The evidence of history, I say, is invaluable in its place; but, if it assumes to be the sole means of gaining religious truth, it goes beyond its place. We are putting it to a larger office than it can undertake, if we countenance the usurpation; and we are turning a true guide and blessing into a source of inexplicable difficulty and interminable doubt.[12]

It must also be noted that this observation, though made in an era of popular writers of history, was before the decades seen as the foundation period for the academic discipline in Britain and at a time when Victorian religious fervour seemed to be at its peak.

Almost a century later, Herbert Butterfield agreed that history should not be used in place of religion. As he stated in *Christianity and History* (1949), "Those who complain that technical history does not provide people with the meaning of life are asking from an academic science more than it can give."[13] Thus, it would appear that MacMillan's observation has a Christian provenance to it. Yet, surprisingly, there has been a measure of rare secular agreement with Butterfield's view. G.N. Clark, Regius Professor of History at Cambridge 1943–7, in his inaugural address, argued for the down-to-earth nature of historical work and stated that history should be no substitute for religion. Alan Bullock of Oxford echoed the same sentiments and made the same point almost a decade later.[14]

Not entirely surprisingly, some treated this area of seeming agreement with suspicion. For example, Herbert Butterfield, in a distrustful mood, believed that some fair-minded historians had "caught heresy from the secular liberals who, having deposed religion, set up scholarship in its place and unduly exalted it, assuming that the academic historian was fitted above all others to provide out of his technique an interpretation of life on the earth."[15] Whether Butterfield ultimately believed this of all historians, especially those beyond the confines of universities, is unclear.

So is MacMillan's observation, an observation prophesied by a number of both religiously minded and secular scholars in the past, an accurate reflection of reality? Is "History" becoming a substitute for religion in the modern world? In order to answer that question, some distinctions must be made. Assuming that MacMillan is addressing a predominantly Western audience, where secularization is most evident, her observation would seem to be born out. As a substitute, one cannot think of any other phenomenon with such mass appeal. Science, a close rival, would still be a framework of belief appealing to a more restricted number of adherents. In the early twentieth century, for example, Julian Huxley had envisaged a secular religion of evolutionary (or scientific) humanism replacing Christianity in the Western world, but its actual core adherents would undoubtedly have been, initially at least, a formally educated minority.[16]

If this potential mass support is conceded, what of the messages so conveyed? Does history set values and standards of a moral nature? Does it show us good from evil in the process? To the "global village," to use McLuhan's terminology, television, the

Internet, and books attempting to capture a mass audience appear to do this. Consciously or subconsciously, history reflects a general set of values described by New Atheist and scientist Richard Dawkins as the moral zeitgeist.[17] This consists of a set of do's and don't's that can be found in the rock-bottom values accepted by a range of people, from adherents of the main-line churches to humanists. For Dawkins, this moral zeitgeist, rather than the dictates of churches, has long dictated decent behaviour (it is in the memes). On the other hand, main-line churches would see this zeitgeist as originating with them or as embedded in divinely inspired natural law. The origins are really not the question. It would be a consensus regarding behaviour rejected only by those at the fringes, from the proverbial mad scientist to ISIS.

In the actual writing of history, there are numerous illustrations of this consensus. Perhaps we can start with the broadest of history – the survey of Western and global history. Shared by public readership and at the most primary college level, it is framed into an explicit narrative – the form also taken by the sacred texts of the Abrahamic religions. From the beginnings of the human race (with liberal doses of anthropology), the narrative goes on to the origins of organized communities and then through a series of attempted larger units to civilizations, the criteria for such a classification varying, but often including a written language. Here, Toynbee is often referred to for his mechanism for the production of a civilization, which, as we have seen, is called either adversity theory or challenge and response. From stable agriculture, to the manifestation of a more sophisticated organization needed for massive projects like irrigation, to occupational specialization, the success of these civilizations seemed to hinge on successful responses to challenges of various sorts, provided they are not over- or under- challenged. Religions sanctioning chain of command, goals, and discipline were a common cultural feature. A rough line of progress through repeated collapses of these civilizations leads to the modern world, with, until recently, emphasis on the almost unique success of Western civilization. A linear progressive view has predominated in the standard story to the present, including the expansion into a global narrative. In a merging world, the forces of economic integration and cultural tolerance are shown to be important factors. A bias towards liberal rationalism can frequently be detected, even in the treatment of religion, which is given its fair share as an important cultural component. In the latter case, pride of place is awarded to those religions that appeal to reason above the mere comforts of emotion.

Bad behaviour is displayed as significant deviance from these trends as well as violations of the moral zeitgeist. In narratives of more specific times and places, there is a greater tendency to extract moral lessons from various developments, with the introduction of a more exacting analysis of social costs of inhumane actions by one group against another. Crude nationalism in national narratives has almost disappeared, with some noteworthy exceptions such as American exceptionalism (no doubt in lineage traceable to Manifest Destiny in the nineteenth century) in US history. Generations earlier, it could regularly be found in the national histories of Britain, Germany, and Russia. In the last case, it might be reappearing in some school texts in the post-Soviet Putin era.

To return to the most general surveys, there remains a dearth of themes or mechanisms to hold such vast narratives together. Economic forces, or combinations or economics and biology such as the Columbian Exchange for Atlantic communities, among the most elemental of factors, seem to be insufficient beyond short-range determinism in the area of politics and diplomacy. With the linear-progressive view increasingly challenged in its specific details, with accusations of bias towards Christianity or liberal rationalism in its overall design, the swelling tide of facts from all continents is simply overwhelming for most readers.

This raises the possibility of a return to some form of metahistory last seen in the 1960s. In the world of historical fiction, often mixed with science fiction, this broader approach has had no difficulty in attracting audiences. It has been good entertainment, of course. Seeing past, present, and future in a continuum has often has served to raise alarm in the public about current trends, particularly through dystopias – a very popular genre. But it also reveals the need to comprehend history as a whole as much as the search for meaning, both of which should be of concern to more members of the academy.

In entering or re-entering the world of metahistory, one cannot avoid the work of Toynbee. Trevor-Roper's famous attack on the *Study of History* conceded that, while it had "not been well received the professional historians," "it has been hailed by the unprofessional public, at least in America, as 'an immortal masterpiece,' 'the greatest work of our time.'" He added, "As a dollar-earner, we are told, it ranks second only to whisky."[18]

In Chapter 3, I presented the thrust of Trevor-Roper's assertion that Toynbee had, in the culmination of his historical study of twenty-one world civilizations, turned himself into a messiah – in positing the emergence of a final Universal Church leading to the end of history. Pieter Geyl's critique, while more restrained, arrived at much the same conclusion – that Toynbee was the prophet of a spiritual process through history leading to the unity of humankind with God. For this reason, for Trevor-Roper, Geyl, and most other academic historians, it was not a proper historical work. In that chapter, I also sampled some of the reactions to the publication of the final volumes of Toynbee's *Study* from other professional historians and selected, broader elements of the educated reading public. In denying that he was some sort of religious prophet and insisting on his overall empirical approach, Toynbee felt that, as a historian, he had supplied his readership with what they needed to comprehend global history. This was not, if we accept Toynbee at his word, primarily a substitute for religion in a Margaret MacMillan sense. Rather, Toynbee saw the key as an emphasis on the cultural influence of world religions past and present. But Toynbee went much further than this, was not accepted at his word, and saw his reputation as a historian systematically destroyed. Certainly in his *Study* we had his version of ultimate meaning revealed in the last volumes, morality applied to global history, and a seeming adherence to truth throughout. These elements would constitute a substitute for religion and much more. For wide audiences, such certainties must have been comforting to read in the rapidly changing postwar world with colonial empires collapsing and the new threat of nuclear annihilation. Certainly a comforting effect can be a characteristic of religion. The power of the academy eventually severed his hold on the public as part of the process of ending the academic credibility of his greatest work.

Toynbee's credibility among scholars was ended by his mystical experiences through time; his professed agnosticism and syncretism, which somehow awarded Christianity the top position for the final path to God; his claim to have researched thoroughly unbelievably huge masses of history encompassed in his study; and his insistence to the end that he was acting as a professional historian. Related to this reaction was an inability to completely win over any significant group such as Christian thinkers (though some remained quite sympathetic) while thoroughly alienating liberal rationalists among others, which left him without any strong support within the academic establishment. The reading world at the time showed sufficient deference to the academy to go along with its final verdict.

Was it possible that some contemporary of Toynbee's could have had better luck in presenting a central thread to all history? Christopher Dawson, if blessed by better health, might have attempted it. He appeared to have had a better mastery than Toynbee of existing research methodology in his metahistory. Dawson's *The Dynamics of World History* (1957) displayed a strong advocacy of modern social science in the form of anthropology and sociology. He also managed to maintain a good dialogue between his metaphysics and the earthly world of professional history. Nevertheless, the *Times Literary Supplement* review saw this work, in keeping with his others, as that of the "most distinguished" of "amateur scholars."[19] His lack of academic status and his strong religious views were well known. As a European cultural historian, he was probably among the best. But his staunch Catholicism, though open to some mixing with other world religions, would always prove to be his Achilles heel among reviewers.

So, is it possible for some sort of metahistory to emerge today that could work? The answer would not be in Harari's *Homo Sapiens*, which is thoroughly materialist and denies meaning in history. In the realm of religion, where History is to function as a substitute, there is opportunity, as I have suggested earlier, but also complication. Secularization, though by no means a fait accompli in the eyes of many experts, has advanced in the Western world since the 1960s. The somewhat stronger position of Christianity in the 1960s than today also posed a strong rival for the potential audience for Toynbee's vaguely theist message. On the other hand, secularization has not been the pattern in other parts of the world. The resurgence of Islam, particularly among youth in parts of the Middle East, Asia, and Africa, not to mention the advance of Christianity in Africa, holds out much less hope for some sort of syncretic universal church substitute proposed by Toynbee.

A more likely case might be made for science. Here the advances since the 1960s, particularly in the areas of neuroscience and the environment, have been staggering. (And, even in the 1960s, Toynbee's knowledge of science was inadequate.) Today science can provide another measure of truth.

For New Atheist scientists such as Richard Dawkins and Sam Harris, who would view Harari as too materialist, one could predict future historical narratives displaying a linear progressive pattern from the Big Bang to wherever the human race finds itself in the present, projecting eras of greater knowledge. Moral progress in this continuum would be measured in terms of an increasing flow of collective achievements. "Sin" would be equated with wilful deviance from the pattern. Such an approach would also be based on greater understanding of ourselves with advances in neuroscience. In this scenario, traditional religion would wither away. As in Julian Huxley's religion of evolutionary humanism, we would not have to face the specter of a rudderless universe. Ideally, we – that is, humanity (or its representatives) – would take the rudder as a replacement for God, the latter passing the baton in an overlapping of dying religion and emergent substitute with no carnage. In the ensuing narrative, historians would supply explanations for past mistakes, which would often have a common cause in fear and excessive selfishness. More refined codes of conduct would follow.

Apart from Harari, how likely is it that such an all-embracing history of humanity originating in this new authority would appear in the near future? It would be anyone's guess. Initially it would be specific to the Western world for a generation to two. The non-Western world would probably be very hostile in its present situation. But we have seen surprises before, such as the rapidity of the collapse of the quasi-religion of Euro-Communism after 1989.

Elements of the new narrative are already in place. Certainly, in public discourse, it would be an important subtext for the atheist-agnostic narrative of history. It also stands side by side with existing narrative religious texts of adherents to Abrahamic traditions, supplemented by special readings of these narratives of the Old and New Testament and the Koran by zealots. General narratives by both have also become a crowded field, especially on cable television and the Internet.

Prayer has been an element in most world religions in explaining how bad things might be contained and a means to increase the frequency of good over evil happenings in individual lives. Without a deity that is independent of ourselves, can there be prayer? Perhaps a practical step is to minimize the situations requiring alleged divine intervention. Without the concept of God, and remnants of Providence, why prayers are not answered also can be readily explained in secular minds. But much of this sounds too rationalistic – the dry, unreadable sort of material the public associates with the academy. As Malcolm Muggeridge once said of his primitive socialist and agnostic childhood, it had an emotional sense of community through devices such as hymns.

What one should hope for in a new, secular treatment of history is emotion, surely one of the prime ways of usurping the role of religion that has never been effectively employed by academics. Both in the passionate presentation of history and in the evoking of emotional responses, history outside the academy has generally been in sharp contrast with that which has been found within the academy. Such passion can be seen in such depictions as Mel Gibson's *The Passion of the Christ* (2004). It is equally seen in Steven Spielberg's *Schindler's List* (1993) where the outrage of inhumanity can exceed any particular religious narrative. Measured by box office sales, it works!

As noted in Chapter 2, Lord Acton once stated that the moral code gave history "its authority, dignity and utility" – without it, history "ceases to be a science, an arbiter of controversy." He also made the observation that history, of itself, "may be used to subjugate or to emancipate – to close enquiry or to promote it."[20] The range of activities in this category of history as a tool is indeed very wide. It could include the use of a narrative for a religion similar to that of the Abrahamic religions. It could include the construction of sweeping national histories to inspire patriotism. At the same, time, it could include the creation of false narratives, even those entailing the rejection of established historical facts such as the Holocaust. It could also include works where the selection of facts supports a range of causes – many very noble, from women's rights to the eradication of slavery.

In the realm of history, a wide array of cults has also appeared, often displaying the theme of destiny. In the secular realm, such cults can represent the equivalent of the lexicon of saints and martyrs. This approach has been associated with figures such as Abraham Lincoln and Winston Churchill. Oddly, it can be found employing some of the same techniques from the "dark side" once used by the followers of Hitler or the leaders of North Korea today. Hitler's Thousand Year Reich paralleled concepts such as the Third Rome in Russian history. Such manipulations of history in a continuum with the future have been suitably shown to be dangerous, along with the existing dangers in any system of thought when taken to extremes. Dystopia, a corrective to much of this, is best seen in some of the later writings of H.G. Wells and, of course, in George Orwell's *Nineteen Eighty-Four* (1948). These are also in the proud tradition of the moral lessons once found even in that staunch advocate of the new discipline of history – William Stubbs.

In the realm of entertainment, which MacMillan notes can be a characteristic of religion today, at least for Evangelicals,[21] many television and movie depictions of past events, whether in docudrama form or outright fiction, remain essentially morality lessons.

At the most elementary level, the search for truth remains a constant feature of history-related activity by those outside academia, from the search for a proper genealogical record of ancestry for the purposes of Mormonism to the perennial search for the truth behind the assassination of John F. Kennedy. In the long run, all of this activity as part of today's history craze must ultimately depend on the integrity of the historian and his or her avoidance of its misuse for public use or private belief. This, I believe, necessitates "keeping faith" with the truth.

Further Observations

I began this section of the book by posing the question of whether or not historians and their readers beyond the academy had shown interest in the questions of truth, morality, and meaning in history. The answer seems to be that they have not wilfully avoided these questions or constructed any theoretical barrier to them. We also noted that, in the case of Toynbee, they were strong supporters of the most ambitious academic attempt to find meaning in history. Many works in popular history openly deal in moral judgment, and there seems to be a stronger belief in seeking the truth – or at least the assumption that it can be found. It must be said that popular history in book or other media forms acts in a pragmatic way to reach market potential and satisfy the public. It is often more open about the espousal of causes and betrays a heavy degree of emotion.

There are activities of the history world beyond what has been discussed here that are also outside the formal realm of the academy. There has always been the area of applied history. For many generations, historians have worked in museums and other areas of the heritage business and have shared the work of librarians in creating and maintaining archives of various sorts. Some positions are extremely distinguished, as in the case of the Librarian of Congress. People in such positions have served as special consultants to tribunals of law, as in the settling of Indigenous land claims in Canada and the United States or in the consulting agencies reviewing civics-history textbooks, for example. And they can be drafted into service in times of special need, as illustrated in the film *The Monuments Men* (2014), depicting, in a fictional version, art historians enlisted by the US government during the Second World War to recover art treasures looted by the Nazis.

A hybrid created by university history departments in recent years called "public history," designed specifically to serve needs outside the academy, has received some attention. James M. Banner, the eternal optimist and encourager of adaptability by young professionals, has admitted that there has been difficulty in defining the position and status of public historians, especially in relation to their academic counterparts.[22] But the field has certainly provided opportunities for newly minted historians with postgraduate credentials to find jobs using their specific training beyond the decreasing number of full- and part-time positions at universities and colleges. Their potential employers from all walks of life, but especially private sector companies, must also appreciate that the ready-made skills of these historians would otherwise have had to have been acquired by regular employees in the course of researching and writing their institutional histories. The field also has tended to create the markets for long-overdue company, church, or even university histories.

The issue of the "hired gun" invariably comes up in these situations. Banner argues that, in serving their "clients," public historians face no more pressure to shade their opinions in service of these clients than do academics in serving ideological causes or the demands of mentors and peers within the academy.[23] However, it must be countered that public historians, by nature of the necessity of their livelihood, are more apt to be placed under obligations of a contractual nature. Often histories so written are forms of public relations or advertising. They can be deemed unsatisfactory by their employers for not achieving goals that go beyond a good narrative to please large audiences: they can fail in their efforts to present a favourable view of the past activities of a corporation, for example, or its brief against protest groups, as in the case of energy companies.

Beyond the ethical/moral questions involved in research and writing can be the criticism that public historians frequently fail to address broad issues of "sustained intellectual discourse."[24] Whether this is altogether a fair criticism is another question. Certainly it has been made by academics, but can it not also be said of many, especially younger, overworked university historians who are forced to keep their noses to the grindstone turning out works of very narrow intellectual appeal?

With public historians, both their roles as originally conceived, and the practical problems of getting on with their tasks, would work against prolonged considerations of the overall meaning of history and theoretical issues about making moral judgments. The pursuit of truth would or should be their most immediate concern. With all the many and varied activities of those involved in dispensing history to the general public, the particular function performed will dictate how much involvement they can have with these broader questions.

To conclude, Fritz Stern made, I believe, the best observation for all those who engage in reconstructions of the past:

> While [the historian's] obligation to the past, his complete, unassailable fidelity to it, must always claim his first loyalty, he must accept the fact that the choices he makes as a historian are not of consequence to him alone, but will affect the moral sense, perhaps the wisdom, of his generation. And since he knows that his own being, his intellectual capabilities and his critical faculties as well as his deeper sense of righteousness and love, are engaged in the writing of history, he knows that his work, too, is a moral act.[25]

Suggested Readings

James M. Banner Jr., *Being a Historian: An Introduction to the Professional World of History* (Cambridge: Cambridge University Press, 2012)

Jack Dougherty and Kristen Nawrotzki eds., *Writing History in the Digital Age* (Ann Arbor: University of Michigan Press, 2013)

Bernard Lewis, *History: Remembered, Recovered, Invented* (Princeton: Princeton University Press, 1975)

Margaret MacMillan, *The Uses and Abuses of History* (Toronto: Penguin, 2008)

Michel-Rolph Trouillot, *Silencing the Past: Power and the Production of History* (Boston: Beacon Press, 1995)

Conclusion

Peter Novick once wrote that, in the sixties, after some small surge in interest in the deepest issues of historiography as seen in the launching of the journal *History and Theory*, "concern with the cognitive foundations of the historical venture was formally ghettoized as an esoteric concern, like business history or the history of South Dakota."[1] Indeed, what Novick described as the pride in being "objective," seeking the designation "definitive" for what was published, and concentrating on business as usual in delivering an account of the past "as it was," remained the way the vast majority of historians approached their task. Novick spoke for the United States, but many of his comments could apply to the profession in Canada and the United Kingdom, if not the rest of the Western world.

My own experience in the sixties had been in researching Victorian English cotton towns, where the new wave of social history focused some of its best efforts on similar projects being about "ordinary chaps." Some of the theories employed in the research may have been derived from sociologists and the like, but the application was thoroughly Rankean. Indeed it was not uncommon for prominent historians such as J.H. Hexter to display pride in being openly ignorant of philosophy and other disciplines in the service of historians' good old common sense.

In 2002, a collection entitled *What Is History Now?* appeared, with the purpose of assessing how things had changed for historians since the publication of E.H. Carr's *What Is History?* some forty years earlier. Under the editorship of David Cannadine, a bevy of historians, mostly British, were assembled to examine how the profession had evolved, both in general terms and in very particular fields (religious, gender, cultural, and so on), with a view to the impact of Carr's ideas as well as to developments as a whole. The volume dealt first with the initial lurch among younger historians towards social history with a bottom-up view of history, away from its obsession with high politics and diplomacy. Most of us in the new wave saw history as a social science, as suggested by Carr. In the process, new subjects of research were introduced, including racial and linguistic minorities.

In the 1980s, the discipline was hit by the impact of Foucault and the linguistic turn, experiencing influences that had already affected other disciplines such as literature. It resulted in emphasis on cultural history, as well as a sharp increase in women's and gender history and many other specialties developed since the 1960s, with linguistics and anthropology being predominant influences. Specialization proliferated with new perspectives, which met with as much hostility as enthusiasm. Nevertheless, individual historians in the Cannadine collection attested to advances in every field, including older areas such as political history. Ideological disarray, however, remained a characteristic of more recent times, often dominating particular fields.

The net result of these trends could be depicted in many ways. Richard J. Evans in the prologue to Cannadine's volume lauded the broad appeal of history beyond the academy, seeing the new academic thinking as one driving force: "Without Hayden White, no David Starkey; without postmodernism, no Simon Schama."[2] For others, such as Felipe Fernandez-Armesto in his epilogue, fragmentation was the price paid for too much specialization in academic circles; and, as far as the growing history world outside academia, he saw television academics playing "bit-parts."[3] The greatest growth area, interest in genealogy, bore little relationship to the academy and therefore the latter could take no credit for it.

The growth of specialties and subspecialties became increasingly linked to being "professional" – a tendency associated with the physical and social sciences. This was reinforced by the way

Conclusion 129

research was done. Funding agencies, using science as their model, encouraged algorithms, to use Harari's favourite term, in the way methodology was presented. This approach, in turn, was reinforced by university administrators anxious to increase their rankings in research success to attract other funding and more students.

In time, graduate schools, wishing to give their graduates the best chance at obtaining and keeping academic positions, included initiatives for securing grants as part of their training. The result, for undergraduates, was the expansion of highly specialized courses and fewer and fewer compulsory or survey "core" or "bread and butter" courses. As R.I. Moore has described it, "professionalism was eating its children."[4] In many cases, especially at smaller universities, the selection of available courses was of much more interest to the instructors than to their undergraduate students – though individual courses could be very attractive to some (and not at all to others). Enrolments in such cases suffered, thus weakening the profile of departments in their attempts to widen their appeal.

As Novick has described the situation for historians in the United States, if not North America as a whole, "History's epistemological crisis was played out against a background of depression which was both material and moral."[5] The timing could not have been worse.

In Canada, highly specialized areas of social history received criticism in the 1990s from the late Michael Bliss and J.L. Granatstein. Both were established academics who produced volumes that reflected their special research interests with an eye to both students and the general public. In his *Who Killed Canadian History?* (1998), Granatstein went further in airing the discord that arose when strong advocates of these new areas undermined the traditional national narrative and the collegiality of academic ranks.

More recently, some peace has seemingly returned, based on the clear need for balance in taking into account newer areas of historical investigation with sufficient respect offered to the older "elites" within academic circles who emphasized political and constitutional matters. In the last regard, it must be said that polemics and discord are of no help in strengthening the appeal of history to students and public alike. Good history starts with a good story, whether in the discovery of insulin or the construction of a more rounded national narrative.

In Continental Europe, and France in particular, the new history inspired by the founders of the Annales school encouraged more integrated work in an interdisciplinary fashion. The annaliste search for "total history" led to a more coherent approach to the wider framework of history. As Moore has explained, a more successful approach to world history could be explored employing the comparative method. Yet, as he has pointed out for the English-speaking world, neither the annalistes nor the best of Marxist analysis had much to do with the recent emergence of world history. It was more a pragmatic affair having to do with a greater awareness of the world about us.[6]

That awareness has come to historians both directly and indirectly through the wider world of history beyond the academy. The sweep of history has always interested the public. Technological advance, including the public embrace of the Internet, has affected both research itself and the presentation of its results. In research, the digitization of some library collections (though there is still a vast amount of laborious work to be done there) has made research online possible for both professors and the public, as we have seen. Availability of sources has also influenced the classroom environment, replacing the early audio-visual aids dating back to the 1950s, the portable television sets in the 1970s, and the VCRs of the 1980s with online visual presentation and Power Point lectures. Again algorithms have been built in by publishers, from online versions of textbooks to teaching and marking packages for instructors. These trends have led to the advance of some fields, like material history, but problems for others, such as intellectual history, that are less adaptable.

Online courses now embrace a steadily increasing percentage of courses offered to both part-time and regular students. Electronic interaction through social media is fostering less face-to-face contact between instructors and students in the traditional classroom. Public libraries engaged in services such as providing resource centres are increasingly becoming gathering places filled with computers rather than books and journals. This, in turn, has led to digital archiving, along with new forms of storage vulnerability and decomposition, as described by Douglas Coupland in *Bit Rot* (2015). Publishers are increasingly facing economic challenges in producing books and journals in the traditional way for academics and the general public alike.

Reliance on the digital world has made sources like Wikipedia a major reference work for both the general public and college students. Both the Net and social media have seen a huge advance in the availability of information. Unfortunately, this unregulated environment has also seen proliferation of disinformation, "fake news," and, most recently, "alternative facts" employed so readily by politicians.

In relation to the main questions in this book, this situation raises both new concerns as well as possible benefits. As stated at the outset, my hope is that history and the study of religion might experience an end to the wall of separation that has existed between them for generations. As C.T. McIntire has pointed out, it could enrich both.[7] Certainly history has drawn first from social psychology and sociology, then anthropology, and then linguistics in recent years to provide new approaches to the discipline. Why is it not possible for a rapprochement with religion, considering centuries ago, and in many cultures today, the friendly relations that were and are a feature of intellectual life for the two areas of study.

There is no need for historians to enter into the debate within many university religious studies departments concerning the nature and definition of religious studies today. As described in Russell McCutcheon's *Critics not Caretakers: Redescribing the Public Study of Religion* (2001), those who seek to make religious studies more of a social science discipline have disagreements with those who see these departments as custodians of religious traditions. My suggestion is that historians should use religious insights to enrich the study of history. This would include considering the feelings and emotions of those adhering to religious cultures as well as the beliefs themselves. Doing so would do much to widen the lens of history, which for so long has focused on the secular and the rational.

Too much time has been spent in debates about the benefits of the barrier defending fortress history, not enough on the benefits of tearing it down. At the same time, one should not expect too much. Sam Harris's hope, in *The Moral Landscape* (2010), for a merger of ethical systems is too optimistic. Even Jürgen Habermas's notion that participants in rational discourse should reach agreements seems unattainable. I believe the solution has to extend beyond merely redefining terms on a piecemeal basis and improving methodology, as suggested by writers such as Alan Munslow in *The Future of History* (2010). As Walter Bagehot once observed of the English, "We are born with a belief in a green cloth, clean pens, and twelve men with grey hair. In topics of belief the ultimate standard is the jury."[8] Committees, in my view, are not the answer. At the same time, I have no sweeping answer to all the questions – no deus ex machina. Each area – truth, morality and meaning – requires some rethinking, with the last, perhaps, providing ultimate hope for them all.

In the short run, truth potentially would seem the most attainable, as the discussion has been most active, but has met with many obstacles, some of recent origin. Truth in history is reliant on accurate facts as well as judgments in separating "historical facts" from other facts, and many considerations arise in determining "historical fact." Was a "fact" originally orally transmitted or was it in written form from the beginning? If it was contained in an account of something or someone, do we know anything about the document producers, their viewpoint, or even why they produced the documents in the first place? Or was the "fact" in the form of material history? If so, was this item thought to be historically significant at the time of its creation? And what of the many stages before the item actually fell into the hands of the historian? There are so many ways in which its authenticity could be questioned, even before the historian applies his or her manipulations of the evidence. Notions of absolute truth resulting from such an imperfect process are doubtful to say the least. Yet are there not times when a reasonableness in judgment based on evidence seems sufficient to allow the historian to move on the next stage in building narratives and drawing conclusions?

Or course, there can be serious reminders of how truth can be distorted, presumably in the service of some ideology. The David

Abraham case in the early 1980s received great attention in the profession. Abraham's revised version of his 1977 University of Chicago PhD thesis was published by Princeton University Press in 1981. The thesis-book contained a strong Marxist argument on the links between industrialists and Nazis in the Weimar Republic. While most of the reviews were favourable, Henry Turner at Yale was strongly critical of his use of evidence, including Abraham's use of allegedly non-existent documents. The controversy spilt into the decision of the Princeton administration to not accept the History Department's recommendation to grant Abraham tenure. Turner was soon joined by Gerald Feldman of Berkeley, and the whole affair went public. Accusations on the part of Turner increased to the level of attack in which Abraham was accused of deliberately publishing falsehoods.

The supporters of Turner became more adamant in demanding suitable punishments but were opposed by historians who felt the errors were of a more minor, mundane nature. Counter-attacks against Turner and Feldman's conduct reached into demands for an investigation by the council of the American Historical Association. The public was brought into the picture by the *New York Times*. As Peter Novick has stated concerning the result, "Turner and Feldman triumphant and Abraham out of the profession … was a striking demonstration of the continued power of the empiricist-objectivist alliance."[9]

Such a situation was less likely to occur in the world of history beyond the academy. However, the opposite situation seems the hazard in the era of "post-truth." Deliberate destruction of records and the like had been the action of many dictators and warring factions in service of both propaganda and disinformation for a very long time. Today wilful disregard of facts readily available in the media of modern democracies and their replacement with "alternative facts" (falsehoods) is a growing trend by some politicians and their associates. It presents a threat to the generosity of spirit in the ready acceptance of facts taken as truths by the general reading public and may explain the sudden renewal of mass interest in George Orwell's *Nineteen Eighty-Four*.[10] Certainly in the present era of "post-truth," the activities of Orwell's Ministry of Truth seem especially relevant.

The issue of moral judgment has been constantly kept in check in the service of producing objective, "scientific" history. But the cost of avoidance can leave the field, especially beyond the academy, to the likes of Holocaust deniers or apathy. As William Dray has observed, unlike scientists and philosophers, historians "endeavor to locate things in their contexts."[11] He has also stated that the historian is not necessarily confined to what was thought to be important in the past, for the historical judgment is being rendered in the present. For example, most people in the summer of 1969 thought the moonwalk was one of the most important events of history. Yet it can be argued by a historian today that the inception of the Internet a few months later at the engineering department of UCLA has had a far more important global impact. Acton, I think, made a good point in stating that, when the facts are known, moral judgments may have to be rendered. But in the course of further research, an appeal process is also possible.

Lastly, on the question of meaning, in my view the answer can only be attempted by the production of great overviews of history. With the publication of Harari's *Homo Sapiens* and *Homo Deus*, the long silence after Toynbee has finally been ended. While very impressive in their execution, Harari's works represent an extreme in their insistence on the non-meaning of human history. As I have suggested, there needs to be a theist challenge at the other end of the spectrum in the spirit of a rapprochement with the study of religion. At the very least, it is time that historians make a serious effort to use religious insights after similar forays into the social sciences and linguistics. Such an effort should also address the questions of truth and morality en route. In an even broader context, a discussion of truth, morality, and meaning might allow the great sprawling mass of historians in various specialties and subspecialties to consider what constitutes the role(s) of the historian in a more pointed way.

Suggested Readings

David Cannadine, ed., *What Is History Now?* (Basingstoke, UK: Palgrave Macmillan, 2002)

Notes

Introduction

1 Michael Bentley, "General Introduction," *Companion to Historiography*, edited by Michael Bentley (London: Routledge, 1997), xii.
2 Ibid.
3 Paul T. Phillips, *The Controversialist: An Intellectual Life of Goldwin Smith* (Westport CT: Praeger, 2002), 24.
4 Bentley, "Introduction: Approaches to Modernity," 444.
5 James M. Banner Jr., *Being a Historian: An Introduction to the Professional World of History* (Cambridge: Cambridge University Press, 2012), 104.
6 Ibid.
7 R.I. Moore, "World History," in Bentley, *Companion to Historiography*, 943.
8 Banner, *Being a Historian*, 251.
9 E.H. Carr, *What Is History?* 2nd ed. (London: Penguin Books, 1987), 75.
10 Peter Novick, *That Noble Dream: The "Objectivity Question" and the American Historical Profession* (Cambridge: Cambridge University Press, 1988), 600.
11 Ibid., 574.
12 J.B. Conacher, "Graduate Studies in History in Canada: The Growth of Doctoral Programmes" (Canadian Historical Association Report, 1975).
13 James Grossman, "History Isn't a 'Useless Major,'" *Los Angeles Times*, 30 May 2016.
14 Banner, *Being a Historian*, 198.
15 C.T. McIntire, "Transcending Dichotomies in History and Religion," *History and Theory* 45, no. 4, "Religion and History" issue (2006): 80–92.
16 Isaiah Berlin, "Does Political Theory Still Exist?" *Philosophy, Politics and Society*, 2nd series, edited by Peter Laslett and W.G. Runciman (Oxford: Basil Blackwell, 1969), 1.

1 Truth

1. E.H. Carr, *What Is History?* 2nd ed. (London: Penguin Books, 1987), 75.
2. See http://www.bbc.co.uk/gcsebitesize: truth. It is archived under Religious Studies: knowledge, faith, belief
3. Carr, *What Is History?* 131.
4. Terry Eagleton, *Reason, Faith and Revolution: Reflections on the God Debate* (New Haven, CT: Yale University Press, 2009), 118.
5. Thomas Kuhn, *The Structure of Scientific Revolutions* (Chicago: University of Chicago Press, 1962).
6. Jeremy Popkin, *From Herodotus to H-Net: The Story of Historiography* (New York: Oxford University Press, 2016), 135. Popkin refers to Lynn Hunt's *Politics, Culture, and Class in the French Revolution* (Berkeley and Los Angeles: University of California Press, 1984).
7. Ibid., 7.
8. "My Brain Made Me Do It," *The Nature of Things*, CBC Television, 17 March 2016.
9. Yuval Noah Harari, *Homo Deus: A Brief History of Tomorrow* (Toronto: Penguin Random House, 2016), 187.
10. Leonard Krieger, *Ranke and the Meaning of History* (Chicago: University of Chicago Press, 1977), 4.
11. Jonathan Gorman, *Historical Judgement: The Limits of Historiographical Choice* (Montreal and Kingston: McGill-Queen's University Press, 2008), 107.
12. Krieger, *Ranke*, 385 n53.
13. Wilson H. Coates and Hayden V. White, *The Ordeal of Liberal Humanism: An Intellectual History of Western Europe*, vol. 2 (New York: McGraw-Hill, 1970), 160.
14. Arnold Toynbee and Philip Toynbee, *Comparing Notes: A Dialogue across a Generation* (London: Weidenfeld and Nicolson, 1963), 79.
15. Lord Acton, "Letter to the Contributors to the Cambridge Modern History," *The Varieties of History*, edited by Fritz Stern (Cleveland, OH: Meridian Books, 1956), 247.
16. William Stubbs, "On the Present State of Prospects of Historical Study May 20, 1876," in *Seventeen Lectures on the Study of Mediaeval and Modern History* (Oxford: Clarendon Press, 1900), 65.
17. Novick, *That Noble Dream*, 53.
18. Ibid., 254.
19. Ibid., 255.
20. J.B. Bury, "History as a Science," in Stern, *Varieties of History*, 210.

21 Gorman, *Historical Judgement*, 133.
22 George Wrong, *Historical Study in the University and the Place of Mediaeval History* (Toronto: Bryant Press, 1895), 7.
23 Lord Acton, "Letter to the Contributors," 247.
24 Fritz Stern, Introduction, *Varieties of History*, 26.
25 G.R. Elton, *The Practice of History*, 2nd ed. (Oxford: Blackwell, 2002), 221.
26 Ibid., 80.
27 Ibid., 79.
28 Oscar Handlin, *Truth in History* (Cambridge, MA: Belknap Press of Harvard University Press, 1979), 405–6.
29 Ibid., 405.
30 Michael Bentley, "General Introduction," xiii–xiv.
31 Frederick Cooper, "Postcolonial Studies and the Study of History," *Postcolonial Studies and Beyond*, edited by Ania Loomba et al. (Durham, NC: Duke University Press, 2005), e 402.
32 Novick, *That Noble Dream*, 567.
33 Handlin, *Truth in History*, 414.
34 David Shields, *Reality Hunger: A Manifesto* (New York: Alfred Knopf, 2010), 57.
35 Terry Eagleton, *Reason, Faith and Revolution*, 136.
36 Lawrence Stone, "History and Post-Modernism," *Past and Present*, no. 135 (May 1992): 189.
37 Ibid., 190.
38 Ibid.
39 Callum Brown, *Postmodernism for Historians* (Harlow: Pearson Education, 2005), 168.
40 Ibid., 146–7.
41 Novick, *That Noble Dream*, 573.
42 Northrop Frye, *T.S. Eliot* (Edinburgh: Oliver and Boyd, 1963), 83.
43 T.S. Eliot, "Burnt Norton," *Four Quartets* (New York: Harcourt, 1943), stanza 1, ll. 12–14.
44 Paul Ricoeur, *The Contribution of French Historiography to the Theory of History* (Oxford: Clarendon Press, 1980), 13.

2 Morality

1 E.H. Carr, *What Is History?* 2nd ed. (London: Penguin Books, 1987), 79, 83, 84.
2 Ibid., 77.

3 William Dray, "Philosophy and History," *Companion to Historiography*, edited by Michael Bentley (London: Routledge, 1997), 770, 771.
4 A.C. Grayling, *The God Argument: The Case against Religion and for Humanism* (New York: Bloomsbury, 2013), 186, 187.
5 Ibid.
6 Carr, *What Is History?* 75.
7 J.E. Kirby, "An Ecclesiastical Descent: Religion and History in the Work of William Stubbs," *Journal of Ecclesiastical History* 65, no. 1 (2013): 84–110.
8 Christine Davies, *Permissive Britain: Social Change in the Sixties and Seventies* (London: Pitman, 1975), 3.
9 Lord Acton, "Inaugural Lecture on the Study of History," *Essays on Freedom and Power*, edited by Gertrude Himmelfarb (Cleveland, OH: Meridian Books, 1955), 51.
10 George Wrong, *Historical Study in the University and the Place of Mediaeval History* (Toronto: Bryant Press, 1895), 19.
11 Grayling, *The God Argument*, 187.
12 Ibid., 188.
13 Richard Dawkins, *The God Delusion* (Boston: Houghton Mifflin, 2008), 298.
14 Michael Bentley, *Modern Historiography: An Introduction* (London: Routledge, 1999), 37.
15 Michael Bentley, "Introduction: Approaches to Modernity," in Bentley, *Companion to Historiography*, 421, 423.
16 Acton, "Inaugural Lecture," 42.
17 Lord Acton, *Selected Writing of Lord Acton*, vol. 3, *Essays in Religion, Politics and Morality*, edited by J. Rufus Fears (Indianapolis: Liberty Classics, 1988), 616.
18 Lord Acton, "Acton-Creighton Correspondence," in Himmelfarb, *Essays on Freedom*, 339.
19 Leonard Krieger, *Ranke and the Meaning of History* (Chicago: University of Chicago Press, 1977), 288–90.
20 Gertrude Himmelfarb, *Lord Acton: A Study of Conscience and Politics* (Chicago: University of Chicago Press, 1952), 204.
21 Acton, *Selected Writing of Lord Acton*, 3: 656.
22 Herbert Butterfield, *Lord Acton* (London: Historical Association, 1948), 5.
23 Acton, *Selected Writing of Lord Acton*, 3: 637.
24 Acton, "Acton-Creighton Correspondence," in *Selected Writing of Lord Acton*, 3: 339.
25 Ibid., 3: 336.

26 Acton, *Selected Writing of Lord Acton*, 3: 494.
27 Ibid., 3: 499.
28 Acton, "Acton-Creighton Correspondence," in *Selected Writing of Lord Acton*, 3: 335.
29 Ibid., 3: 335–6.
30 Acton, *Selected Writing of Lord Acton*, 3: 656.
31 Ibid., 3: 616–17.
32 Hugh Tulloch, "Lord Acton and German Historiography, *British and German Historiography, 1750–1950*, edited by Benedikt Stuchtey and Peter Wende (London: Oxford University Press, 2000), 166–7.
33 Roland Hill, *Lord Acton* (New Haven, CT: Yale University Press, 2000), 412.
34 Tulloch, "Lord Acton and German Historiography."
35 Hugh Tulloch, *Lord Acton* (New York: St. Martin's Press, 1986), 87–112.
36 Ibid., 110.
37 Acton, "Letter to Contributors," *The Varieties of History*, edited by Fritz Stern, (Cleveland, OH: World Publishing, 1965), 247–9.
38 Acton, *Selected Writing of Lord Acton*, 3: 582.
39 Acton, "Acton-Creighton Correspondence," letter of 5 April 1887, in *Selected Writing of Lord Acton*, 3: 336.
40 Acton, *Selected Writing of Lord Acton*, 3: 632.
41 *Times* (London), 20 June 1902.
42 Dom David Knowles, *The Historian and Character* (Cambridge: Cambridge University Press, 1963), 13.
43 C.T. McIntire, *Herbert Butterfield: Historian as Dissenter* (New Haven, CT: Yale University Press, 2004), 69.
44 Ibid., 72–3.
45 Herbert Butterfield, "Moral Judgments in History," in *History and Human Relations* (London: Collins, 1951), 116.
46 McIntire, *Herbert Butterfield*, 222.
47 Adrian Oldfield, "Moral Judgements in History," *History and Theory* 20, no. 3 (1981): 277.
48 Jonathan Gorman, "Historians and Their Duties," *History and Theory* 43, no. 4 (2004): 103–17.
49 Carr, *What Is History?* 79.
50 Gertrude Himmelfarb, "Of Heroes, Villains and Valets," Chapter 2 of *On Looking into the Abyss: Untimely Thoughts on Culture and Society* (New York: Alfred A. Knopf, 1994), 27–49.
51 Mark Salber Phillips, *On Historical Distance* (New Haven, CT: Yale University Press, 2013), 193.

52 Paul T. Phillips, *The Controversialist: An Intellectual Life of Goldwin Smith* (Westport CT: Praeger, 2002), 25.
53 Ibid., 30.
54 Ibid., 63.
55 Paul T. Phillips, *Contesting the Moral High Ground: Popular Moralists in Mid-Twentieth Century Britain* (Montreal and Kingston: McGill-Queen's University Press, 2013), 79.
56 Grayling, *The God Argument*, 171.

3 Meaning

1 Marc Bloch, *The Historian's Craft* (New York: Vintage Books, 1953), 194.
2 R.W. Davies, ed., "E.H. Carr's Files: Notes towards a Second Edition of *What Is History?*" in E.H. Carr, *What Is History?* 2nd ed. (London: Penguin Books, 1987), 169–70. In the second edition, the text of the first edition was not revised. Davies's edited notes from Carr's files were added to the end of the book. Carr died in 1982, long before his plan could be realized.
3 Mircea Eliade, *The Myth of the Eternal Return, or, Cosmos and History* (Princeton, NJ: Princeton University Press, 1971), 113.
4 Ibid., 161–2.
5 Ibid., 137.
6 Charles Taylor, *A Secular Age* (Cambridge, MA: Belknap Press of Harvard University Press, 2007), chap. 6.
7 Herbert Butterfield, *Christianity and History* (London: G. Bell and Son, 1949), 95–6.
8 Herbert Butterfield, *History and Human Relations* (London: Collins, 1951), 148, 154.
9 Butterfield, *Christianity and History*, 20–1.
10 Ibid., 107.
11 Butterfield, "The Modern Historian," *Herbert Butterfield: Writings on Christianity and History*, edited by C.T. McIntire (New York: Oxford University Press, 1979), 137.
12 Butterfield, "God in History," in ibid., 5.
13 Butterfield, *Christianity and History*, 94.
14 Butterfield, *History and Human Relations*, 37.
15 See Paul T. Philips, *Contesting the Moral High Ground: Popular Moralists in Mid-Twentieth Century Britain* (Montreal and Kingston: McGill-Queen's University Press, 2013), chap. 2.
16 Butterfield, *Christianity and History*, 4–5.

17 Himmelfarb, "Postmodernist History," Chapter 7 in *On Looking into the Abyss: Untimely Thoughts on Culture and Society* (New York: Alfred A. Knopf, 1994), 155–6.
18 Christopher Dawson, *Progress and Religion: An Historical Enquiry* (London: Sheed and Ward, 1929), 245.
19 Ibid., 244.
20 See Stephen G. Carter, "The 'Historical Solution' versus the 'Philosophical Solution': The Political Commentary of Christopher Dawson and Jacques Maritain, 1927–1939," *Journal of the History of Ideas* 69, no. 1 (2008): 93–115.
21 William H. McNeill, *Arnold J. Toynbee: A Life* (New York: Oxford University Press, 1989), 67–9.
22 Arnold Toynbee, "A Study of History: What I Am Trying to Do," *Toynbee and History: Critical Essays and Reviews*, edited by M.F. Ashley Montagu (Boston: Porter Sargent Publishers, 1956), 3.
23 Arnold Toynbee, "A Study of History, What the Book Is For: How the Book Took Shape," in ibid., 8.
24 H. Stuart Hughes, *Oswald Spengler: A Critical Estimate*, rev. ed. (New York: Charles Scribner's Sons, 1962), 138–42.
25 McNeill, *Arnold J. Toynbee*, 227.
26 Ibid.
27 Ibid.
28 Hughes, *Oswald Spengler*, 146.
29 Christopher Dawson, "The Problem of Metahistory," *History Today* 1, no. 6 (1951): 9.
30 Arnold Toynbee, *A Study of History*, vol. 12, *Reconsiderations* (London: Oxford University Press, 1961), 229.
31 H.R. Trevor-Roper, "Arnold Toynbee's Millennium," *Encounter* 8, no. 6 (1957): 14–28.
32 Pieter Geyl, "Toynbee's System of Civilizations," in Montagu, *Toynbee and History*, 71.
33 Ibid., 68.
34 Pieter Geyl, "Toynbee Once More: Empiricism or Apriorism," Chapter 7 in *Debates with Historians* (London: B.T. Batsford, 1955), 157.
35 Pieter Geyl, "Toynbee the Prophet," Chapter 8 of *Debates with Historians*, 159, 168, 178, 177.
36 Tangye Lean, "A Study of Toynbee," in Montagu, *Toynbee and History*, 37n6.
37 McNeill, *Arnold J. Toynbee*, 256.

38 Christopher Dawson, "Civilizations in History," in Montagu, *Toynbee and History*, 139.
39 Linus Walker, "Toynbee and Religion: A Catholic View," in ibid., 346.
40 Abba Eban, "The Toynbee Heresy," in ibid., 324.
41 McNeill, *Arnold J. Toynbee*, 247.
42 Michael Lang, "Globalization and Global History in Toynbee," *Journal of World History* 22, no. 4 (2011): 747.
43 Kenneth E. Bock, "Review of *A Study of History*: Vol. XII: *Reconsiderations* by Arnold J. Toynbee," *History and Theory* 2, no. 3 (1963): 303–4.
44 C.T. McIntire and Marvin Perry, eds. *Toynbee: Reappraisals* (Toronto: University of Toronto Press, 1989), vii.
45 *History and Theory* 43, no. 4 (2004), 45, no. 4 (2006).
46 Yuval Noah Harari, *Sapiens: A Brief History of Humankind* (Toronto: Penguin Random House, 2014), 240.
47 Ibid., 241.
48 Yuval Noah Harari, *Homo Deus: A Brief History of Tomorrow* (Toronto: Penguin Random House, 2016), 59.
49 Harari, *Sapiens*, 389, 391.
50 Ibid., 86.
51 Ibid., 79.
52 Ibid., 243.
53 Ibid., 166.
54 Harari, *Homo Deus*, 46. The third project "obviously subsumes the first two projects" – that is, to seek immortality (or "amortality," his preferred term) and to find the key to happiness (28).
55 Ibid., 46, 47.
56 Harari, *Sapiens*, 236.
57 Ibid., 210 (emphasis in original).
58 Harai, *Homo Deus*, 184.
59 Ibid., 185.
60 Harai, *Sapiens*, 216.
61 Harari, *Homo Deus*, 181.
62 Harari, *Sapiens*, 314.
63 Harari, *Homo Deus*, 198, 199.
64 Ibid., 98.
65 Ibid., 212.
66 Ibid., 247, 283, 304.
67 Ibid.
68 Ibid., 305.
69 Ibid., 350.
70 Ibid., 351, 380.

71 As described under "Data Religion," 378–80 in ibid.
72 Harari, *Sapiens*, 244.
73 Ibid., 9.
74 Ibid., 21.
75 Ibid., 32, 27.
76 Ibid., 244.
77 Ibid., 168.
78 Harari, *Homo Deus*, 185.
79 Harari, *Sapiens*, 243.
80 Phillips, *Contesting the Moral High Ground*, 58.
81 Bradley J. Birzer, *Sanctifying the World: The Augustinian Life and Mind of Christopher Dawson* (Front Royal, VA: Christendom Press, 2007), 71.
82 Dawson, *Progress and Religion*, 244.
83 Barbara Ward, "Are Today's Basic Problems Religious?" *The Mott Foundation Lectures* (Ann Arbor: University of Michigan Press, 1953), 17, 16, 12.
84 Phillips, *Contesting the Moral High Ground*, 141.
85 Ibid., 152, 153.
86 Quoted in Martin C. D'Arcy, *Humanism and Christianity* (New York: World Publishing, 1969), 15, 120.
87 Martin C. D'Arcy, *The Sense of History: Secular and Sacred* (London: Faber and Faber, 1959), 15.
88 Geoffrey Barraclough, "The Prospects of World History," *The New World History: A Teacher's Companion*, edited by Ross E. Dunn (Boston: Bedford, 2000), 126.

4 History beyond the Academy

1 Acton, Letter to Mary Gladstone, 10 Feb. 1881, in Lord Acton, *Selected Writings of Lord Acton*, vol. 3, *Essays in Religion, Politics and Morality*, edited by J. Rufus Fears (Indianapolis: Liberty Classes, 1988), 642.
2 Acton, Letter to Mary Gladstone, 1 Sept. 1883, ibid.
3 Peter Novick, *That Noble Dream: The "Objectivity Question" and the American Historical Profession* (Cambridge: Cambridge University Press, 1988), 45.
4 Ibid.
5 "Almost 40 Years Later a Miniseries Returns to Television's Roots," *Time*, 30 May 2016.
6 See Tim Hitchcock and Robert Shoemaker, "Making History Online," Colin Matthews Lecture for the Public Understanding of History, 12 Nov. 2014, *Transactions of the Royal Historical Society*, 6th series, 25 (2015): 75–93.

7 Jack Doughtery and Kristen Nawrotzki, *Writing History in the Digital Age* (Ann Arbor: University of Michigan Press, 2013), 22.
8 Ibid., 273.
9 "Oxford Dictionaries Word of the Year 2016 Is ..." https://www.oxforddictionaries.com/press/news/2016/12/11/WOTY-16.
10 Michel-Rolph Trouillot, *Silencing the Past: Power and the Production of History* (Boston: Beacon Press, 1995), 19.
11 Margaret MacMillan, *The Uses and Abuses of History* (Toronto: Viking Canada, 2008), 21.
12 J.H. Newman, *The Idea of a University* (Garden City, NY: Double Day, 1959), 123–4.
13 Herbert Butterfield, *Christianity and History* (London: G. Bell and Sons, 1949), 22.
14 Allan Bullock, "The Historian's Purpose," *History Today* 1, no. 2 (1951): 5–11.
15 Butterfield, *Christianity and History*, 22.
16 See Paul T. Phillips, *Contesting the Moral High Ground: Popular Moralists in Mid-Twentieth Century Britain* (Montreal and Kingston: McGill-Queen's University Press, 2013), chap. 2.
17 Richard Dawkins, *The God Delusion* (Boston: Houghton Mifflin, 2008), 298–308.
18 Hugh Trevor-Roper, "Arnold Toynbee's Millennium," *Encounter* 8, no. 6 (1957): 14.
19 Bradley J. Birzer, *Sanctifying the World: The Augustinian Life and Mind of Christopher Dawson* (Front Royal, VA: Christendom Press, 2007), 259.
20 Acton, *Selected Writings of Lord Acton*, 3: 633.
21 MacMillan, *The Uses and Abuses of History*.
22 James M. Banner Jr., *Being a Historian: An Introduction to the Professional World of History* (Cambridge: Cambridge University Press, 2012), 138.
23 Ibid., 147.
24 Ibid., 140.
25 Fritz Stern, "Introduction," *The Varieties of History*, edited by Fritz Stern (Cleveland, OH: Meridian Books, 1956), 32.

Conclusion

1 Peter Novick, *That Noble Dream: The "Objectivity Question" and the American Historical Profession* (Cambridge: Cambridge University Press, 1988), 593.

2 Richard J. Evans, "Prologue: What Is History? – Now," *What Is History Now?* edited by David Cannadine (Basingstoke: Palgrave Macmillan, 2002), 15.
3 Felipe Fernandez-Armesto, "Epilogue: What Is History Now?" in ibid., 149, 159.
4 R.I. Moore "World History," *Companion to Historiography*, edited by Michael Bentley (London: Routledge, 1997), 945.
5 Novick, *That Noble Dream*, 573.
6 R.I. Moore, "World History," 944–5.
7 C.T. McIntire, "Transcending Dichotomies, in History and Religion," *History and Theory* 45, no. 4 (2006): 80–92.
8 Walter Bagehot, quoted by Norman St. John Stevans, Introduction, *Bagehot's Historical Essays* (Garden City, NY: Doubleday, 1965), xiv.
9 Novick, *That Noble Dream*, 621.
10 The American news network CNN has reported on the novel's reprinting and sales, *CNN Money*, 25 January 2017.
11 William Dray, "Philosophy and History," in Bentley, *Companion to Historiography*, 777.

Index

Acton, Lord: and Cambridge Modern History, 25, 54–5; and Thomas Carlyle, 52, 106; and Catholicism, 47–50, 52–3; and Ignaz Dollinger, 48, 51–2; and *English Historical Review*, 53; on free will, 50–1; and Georg W.F. Hegel, 53; on historical evidence, 25, 27; on liberalism, 52; and Thomas Babington Macaulay, 106–7; on moral code, 51, 55, 99, 122–3, 134; on Providence as progress, 25, 51; on psychological elements, 33; and Leopold von Ranke, 25, 48, 50
alternate history, 112–13
American Historical Association, 11, 12, 14, 26, 133
Augustine, St., 20, 64, 97

Banner, James M., 9, 12, 16, 125
Barraclough, Geoffrey, 103
Bentley, Michael, 5, 7, 8, 29, 46
Berdyaev, Nicholas, 12, 101
Berlin, Isaiah, 17, 58
big history, 86

Bliss, J.M., 108, 129
Bloch, Marc, 3, 62
Brown, Callum, 35
Buckle, Henry Thomas, 7, 26, 66
Buddhism, 77, 82, 89, 97
Bullock, Alan, 79, 116
Burns, Edward McNall, 71
Bury, J.B., 26
Butterfield, Herbert, 5, 30, 43, 51, 56–8, 67–9, 84, 102, 103, 115–16

Carlyle, Thomas, 7, 52, 106
Carr, E.H.: on accident in history, 33, 63; on background of historians, 5; on causation, 33; on goal of history, 12–13; on historical facts, 27, 40, 59; influence of, 127–8; on moral judgment, 40–2, 58–9; on truth, 19–20, 28. See also *What Is History?*
causalism, 43
Chakrabarty, Dipesh, 30
Clark, G.N., 116
Clark, Kenneth, 70, 109
Collingwood, R.G., 27, 69
Comte, August, 7, 60, 66

Cooper, Frederick, 29
counterfactual history, 112
Croce, Benedetto, 27, 41,69
cyclical view of history, 59, 63–4, 82

Darwin, Charles, 94–5
David Abraham case, 132–3
Dawkins, Richard, 46, 60, 90, 102, 117, 121
Dawson, Christopher, 71–3, 79, 82, 97–8, 103, 120
deism, 12, 66
Denial (2016 motion picture), 113
Diamond, Jared, 86, 91
digitization, 109–11, 130
Dilthey, Wilhelm, 27
Dray, W.H., 31, 41, 113, 134
Durant, Ariel, 71
Durant, Will, 71

Eagleton, Terry, 20, 33,
Eastern Orthodoxy, 100–1
Eliade, Mircea, 63–4
Eliot, T.S., 37, 72
Elton, G.R., 28, 33, 38
Enlightenment, the, 6–7, 21, 29, 42, 60, 64, 66, 69–70, 101
Evangelicals, 36, 94–6, 123
Evans, Richard J., 35, 128

Ferguson, Niall, 108, 109, 112
Fogel, Robert, 112
Foucault, Michel, 34, 128
free will, 20, 43, 50–1, 61, 62, 65, 68, 77, 88, 90, 98
Freeman, E.A., 27, 45, 106
French Revolution, 6, 20, 21, 22, 54, 92
Frye, Northrop, 37, 42

Geyl, Pieter, 80–2, 84, 119
Gorman, Jonathan, 26, 58–9

Gorski, Philip S., 102
Granatstein, J.L., 129
Grayling, A.C., 41–2, 45, 61
Green, John Richard, 106
Grossman, James, 15

Haley, Alex, 107–9
Hamerow, Theodore, 17
Handlin, Oscar, 28–30, 33, 38
Harari, Yuval Noah: on the Agricultural Revolution, 87, 90–1; on the Cognitive Revolution, 87, 91; on free will, 88, 90; on history, 86–8; on Homo deus, 88, 92–3; on Homo sapiens, 37, 87–8; on humanism, 90; on liberalism, 90; on morality, 88–9, 91; on religion, 21, 88–90, 93, 102; on the Scientific Revolution, 88, 90, 92; on truth, 20–1, 90–1
Hare, Julius, 23
Harris, Sam, 46, 60, 99, 100, 121, 132
Hegel, Georg W.F., 7, 12, 53, 68–9, 71
Hinduism, 16, 82, 94, 97
Hitchens, Christopher, 102
Hume, David, 22–3, 66
Huxley, Julian, 68, 72, 92–3, 95, 116, 121
Huxley, Thomas (T.H.), 95

Islam, 16, 82, 94, 121

Judaism, 16, 42, 51, 63, 70, 82–3, 94, 96–8

Kant, Immanuel, 24, 66, 68
Knowles, Dom David, 56, 100
Kuhn, Thomas, 20

Leo, Heinrich, 71
Lessing's Ditch, 22
Lewis, C.S., 42, 99

linear progressive view of history, 23, 25, 51, 59–61, 63–4, 66, 96–8, 117–18, 121

Macaulay, Thomas Babington, 7, 51, 106–7
MacMillan, Margaret, 36, 108, 114–24
Marxism, 11, 69
McCutcheon, Russell, 131
McIntire, C.T., 16, 57–8, 84–5, 131
McLuhan, Marshall, 36, 116
Michelet, Jules, 7, 106
Moore, R.I., 9, 129, 130
Munslow, Alan, 36, 132

New Atheism, 36, 38, 46, 60–1, 90, 98–9, 100, 102, 117, 121, 132. *See also* Dawkins, Richard; Harris, Sam; Hitchens, Christopher
Newman, J.H., Cardinal, 49, 99, 115
Novick, Peter, 13, 26, 30, 35, 107, 127, 129, 133

Oldfield, Adrian, 58
original sin, 50, 60, 98
Orwell, George, 36, 123, 133

Phillips, Mark Salber, 59
Popkin, Jeremy, 20
postmodernism, 15, 33–5, 69, 87 128
public history, 15, 125

Ranke, Leopold von, 7–9, 17, 23–30, 33, 36, 38, 46, 48, 50, 54, 56, 66–7, 70–1, 107, 127
Renaissance, 6, 21, 80–1, 83, 101
Ricoeur, Paul, 37–8
Roman Catholicism, 5, 21, 42, 47–50, 52–3, 55, 65, 72–3, 77, 80, 82, 94, 96–100, 120
Russell, Bertrand, 61

Said, Edward, 29
science: history as a form of, 7, 13–14, 25–7, 36, 38, 53, 57, 69, 128; and progress, 6, 20, 44, 60, 66, 88, 101; and religion, 90–1, 94–6, 98, 116, 121, 131
Scott, Sir Walter, 13, 45, 107
Shermer, Michael, 60
Shields, David, 31
Smith, Goldwin, 8, 43–5, 60, 99
Spengler, Oswald, 71–2, 76, 81
Stern, Fritz, 28, 126
Stone, Laurence, 34–5
Stubbs, William, 8, 9, 25–6, 43, 50, 123

Taylor, Charles, 65–6, 95
Telling the Truth about History (Appleby, Hunt, and Jacob), 38
Thompson, E.P., 11, 59, 69
Toynbee, Arnold J.: challenge and response, 76–7, 117; and Christopher Dawson on metahistory, 71, 73, 79–80, 120; on free will, 77; and Pieter Geyl, 80–1, 83, 119; on Jews, 82–3; and Leopold von Ranke, 25; religious ideas, 77–8, 80–2, 93, 119–20; and Oswald Spengler, 76, 81
– and *Study of History*: abridgement by D.C. Somervell, 78; and decline of Western Civilization, 80–2; early plans for, 75–6; first six volumes, 76–7; and the First World War, 74; importance of universal churches, 77–8, 80, 119; reactions to first six volumes, 77; and Hugh Trevor-Roper, 80–1, 83, 119
Trouillot, Michel-Ralph, 19, 114

Vico, Giambattista, 22–3, 36, 64

Ward, Barbara, 72, 94, 97–8
Wells, H.G., 69, 123
What Is History? (Carr), 12, 19, 27, 40, 59, 63, 127
White, Hayden, 25, 36, 128

Wright, Robert, 94
Writing History in the Digital Age (Doughtery and Nawrotski), 110–11
Wrong, George, 26–7, 44–5

www.ingramcontent.com/pod-product-compliance
Lightning Source LLC
Chambersburg PA
CBHW030326080526
44584CB00012B/729